Lunch Box

MARIE BRETON AND ISABELLE EMOND

dieticians

Lunch Box

Creative Recipes
for Everyday
Lunches

Fitzhenry & Whiteside

Lunch Box

2006 First English Translation © Fitzhenry & Whiteside
Originally published in French © 2001, Flammarion Quebec

Fitzhenry and Whiteside Limited
195 Allstate Parkway
Markham, Ontario L3R 4T8

In the United States:
311 Washington Street,
Brighton, Massachusetts 02135

www.fitzhenry.ca   godwit@fitzhenry.ca

Fitzhenry & Whiteside acknowledges with thanks the Canada Council for the Arts, and the Ontario Arts Council for their support of our publishing program. We acknowledge the financial support of the Government of Canada through the Book Publishing Industry Development Program (BPIDP) for our publishing activities.

Library and Archives Canada Cataloguing in Publication
Breton, Marie, 1962–
Lunch box : creative recipes for everyday lunches / Marie Breton & Isabelle
Emond ; translated by Janet Guillard.

Translation of: Boîte à lunch emballante.
Includes index.
ISBN 1-55041-971-4
1. Lunchbox cookery.   I. Emond, Isabelle   II. Guillard, Janet   III. Title.
TX735.B7313 2006   641.5'34   C2006-900674-1

United States Cataloguing-in-Publication Data
Breton, Marie, 1962–
Lunch box : creative recipes for everyday lunches / Marie Breton ; & Isabelle Emond ; translated by Janet Guillard.
Originally published as: Boîte à lunch ; Quebec City, Quebec : Flammarion, 2001.
[190] p. : col. ill., photos. ; cm.
Includes index.
Summary: Recipes to take lunch from the everyday to the fantastic, including a four week meal planner, tips on food handling and preparation, and nutritional information.
ISBN 1-55041-917-4 (pbk.)
1. Lunchbox cookery. I. Emond, Isabelle. II. Title.
641.5/34 dc22   TX735.B74 2006

Design and illustrations by Olivier Lasser
Photos by Louis Desjardins
Styling by Linda McKenty
Accessories from Ares, Baron Sport and Stokes
Printed and bound in Hong Kong

1 3 5 7 9 10 8 6 4 2

Contents

Soups

Dressings, Dips and Sauces

Eggs and pasta

Chicken and Beef

A Thank You!

Writing this book has been a pleasure! It has been so easy for us, due to all of you who have contributed to it with your knowledge, experience and enthusiasm. From the bottom of our hearts we say "thank you".

To Louise Loiselle, our passionate editor, who believed in this project from the beginning and made it fly.

To Marielle Ledoux, Ph.D., professor, Department of nutrition at the University of Montreal who, in spite of a 'sport-focused' schedule, has shared with us her tips on food while training.

To the parents and students of Saint-Emile school in Montreal and to the Sacred Heart boarding school in Saint-Bruno who have given us their food preferences.

To Michel Boudreau, a passionate computer expert who miraculously retrieved some 'lost documents', and for whom the nutritive value calculations for the recipes have been (almost) child's play.

To Victor, Jeanne, and Estelle, Isabelle's children, who have experimented (more than once) with most of the recipes in this book. Thanks to you, our creations have been put to the test and passed successfully! A special thanks to you Victor, for your wonderful suggestions.

To Gabriel and Julien, Marie's sons, whose taste for adventure have given her, besides the good times spent together, the essential practical experience to document this book. When is the next outing guys?

And to Pierre and Charles, our respective partners, thank you for allowing us those many weekends and evenings while we were testing our creations, working at our computers or researching lunch box related items in the department stores. A lunch for two — would that please you?

Introduction
Exciting news!

D o you have the task of preparing, for the children, your partner or yourself, lunches that will go to the office, school, daycare, day camp or holidays? Then you are not alone, since one Canadian in three leaves home with a lunch box under his/her arm! This is not surprising when one reflects on the many advantages of preparing and taking with you a home-made meal.

First, a lunch is economical. It is easy to spend $5 to $10 (tip not included) for a mid-day lunch in a restaurant, when a good homemade lunch costs less than half that with very little effort. When you save $5 a day for a whole year, that's more than $1,300, enough for a week's holiday in the sun, a new computer or a great bike!

Second, when making your lunch one knows what is in it! You can choose the quality and the quantity of food each day according to your taste, hunger level, nutritional needs and time schedule.

Finally, a lunch is practical. It can be eaten when hungry at any time. It can be eaten anywhere — at the cafeteria, in the park, at the desk, while walking, or in the car. Lunch is mobile and handy.

It is true that for a family of four, 5 days a week and 50 weeks per year, there are 1000 nourishing and exciting lunches to prepare! Of course this is not the case for all of us but for a number of us — parents, students and workers — preparing lunches is a routine job which most of us would rather skip.

The good news? Two dieticians, friends and mothers, have decided to share their expertise! In *Lunch Box*, they deliver on a platter proven recipes and strategies used with their families. Their motto: speed, health, and enjoyment. You will find in the following pages:

- **Quick to prepare healthy and appetizing recipes,** from soup to dessert, including vegetarian recipes, recipes which can be made in 15 minutes or less, recipes which can be frozen and eaten hot or cold and recipes which can, for some, be prepared by children. For each recipe, tips and nutritional values per serving are given.

- **Pages of information and advice** are given on nutritional needs of children and adults, choices of lunch boxes, what foods to include, time management, precautions to take when buying and consuming food , including frozen dinners, meal alternatives, and fast-food. These are all presented in small, easy to understand sections, interspersed with easy-to-read lists and tables.

- **Four weeks** of varied and well-balanced menus meant to inspire you.

Ready for adventure? Let's get started! Let our following lunches provide endless variety...

Chapter 1
Let's Get Started!

A performing engine, smooth transmission and low gas consumption are all important when one purchases a car. But a strong body, comfortable interior and reliable equipment are just as important. The same goes for your lunch. No matter how well prepared it is, it will only be fully appreciated if it is surrounded with the best accessories. Who would want a mashed banana, a crushed sandwich, a soggy muffin, warm milk or lukewarm soup? Or worse, be sick from having eaten a contaminated meal? Thankfully, a number of lunch boxes, thermos bottles, and other efficient, practical and inexpensive plastic containers are widely available on the market today. So no more excuses!

Before buying: 6 questions to reflect on

1. **Do I usually bring a complete meal or only part of it, the second part being prepared on the premises?** With the second option, fewer accessories will be necessary and the lunch bag could be smaller.

2. **At work or at school, do I have access to a refrigerator to keep the food cold until meal time?** If yes, the need for thermos bottles and ice packs will be reduced and the lunch bag could be smaller with less insulation required.

3. **Do I have access to a microwave oven to warm up the food at meal time?** If yes, the need for thermos bottles will be less.

4. **Will lunch be eaten several hours after its preparation?** If yes, the quality of the thermos bottles and the insulation of the lunch bag become more important.

5. **Do I prefer to buy my drink, hot or cold, on the premises rather than bring it from the house?** If yes, the thermos bottles may not be necessary.

6. **Who will be the main user of the equipment?** The strength and size of the accessories will depend on it.

Ideal Equipment

- is versatile enough to accommodate a wide variety of menus.
- is large enough to comfortably hold all the food.
- is able to keep food at the proper temperature (hot or cold) and to maintain the food's flavor, texture and nutritional value safely.
- is sufficiently sturdy to take a few knocks.

First the Accessories!

It is best to first acquire the thermos bottles, sealed containers and other pieces of equipment that will fit our needs. We will then choose a box or a bag large enough to hold everything comfortably.

The Thermos Bottle

The word "Thermos" is the name of the trademark of the original manufacturer. Thermos bottles are designed to maintain beverages and food hot or cold for several hours. They are available in plastic, glass or stainless steel, in all sizes and at all prices. It is up to us to choose according to our needs.

SMALL OR LARGE NECK?

The choice of a large or small opening in a thermos bottle depends on its use.

The small neck: it facilitates pouring and limits heat loss. It is ideal for soups and hot and cold beverages.

The large neck: it makes the cleaning of the bottle easier. It is recommended for solid food (soups, salads, ready-made meals) but also can be used for liquids.

PLASTIC THERMOS

They are inexpensive and not as fragile as glass-lined thermoses. One can eat directly from them without fear of damage. Most are insulated with foam, others with glass, and still others with a

combination of foam and glass. Obviously the risk of breakage increases whenever glass is used. Something new: some newer models have a built-in agent which is activated in a microwave oven and continues to produce heat even after the plastic thermos has been removed. One can also reheat the food directly (with the lid off). How efficient are they? It varies depending on the model. Generally speaking, except for those that have been designed for microwave oven use, these bottles are best for beverages and cold food (i.e. juice, milk, salads, and cold ready-made meals).

Their cost? Between $6 and $15 depending on size (between 235 ml and 500 ml).

For whom? Children especially, as plastic thermoses are generally tough.

PRACTICAL: SMALL ROUND THERMOS (235 ML) WITH LARGE OPENING

Great for puddings, fruit salads, yogurts, cold snacks, gelatins, and other desserts. For added efficiency you can cool the lid by placing it in the fridge or freezer overnight.

Cost? Around $3.

GLASS THERMOS BOTTLE

Those of our childhood, affordable but breakable! With time they can become expensive.

How efficient are they? Good but not as good as a stainless steel thermos (see our test on page 12). According to the manufacturers, they keep cold liquids cold for 24 hours and hot liquids hot for 8 to 10 hours.

Their cost? Between $7 and $15 depending on size (between 235 ml and 1 L) and special features (0, 1 or 2 serving cups, space in the cork or in the base to accommodate cream and sugar, etc.). Note:

the cost of a replacement glass liner ranges from $6.50 to $9. In some cases it is 50% more than a new thermos.

For whom? For adults, given their fragility.

STAINLESS STEEL THERMOS

The exterior and interior walls are made of stainless steel and are vacuum insulated. The result is that these bottles are efficient, durable and unbreakable. The only problem is that they can get battered. Some models have a charcoal insulation, which limits the heat loss when a damaged exterior wall is in contact with an interior wall.

Their efficiency? According to the manufacturers, most keep cold liquids cold for 24 to 26 hours and hot liquids hot for 8 to 14 hours (see our test on page 12).

Their cost? Between $15 and $40 depending on size (450 ml to 1.2 L) and features of each one (handle, strap, etc.).

For whom? Mostly for adults, given their high cost, and especially for work or recreational activities.

For maximum efficiency

Cool or heat the thermos before using it. Fill it with iced or boiling water, put the lid on, wait 5 to 10 minutes, and then empty the bottle. One can then pour the beverage or food in the container, ensuring that it is as cold or as hot as possible. Another option for cold food is to leave the thermos, open and empty, to cool overnight in the refrigerator. Then in the morning fill thermos with the cold contents.

WE HAVE PUT THEM TO THE TEST!

This little in-house test gives an idea of the relative efficiency of the thermos bottles that we have just described. We observe that stainless steel thermoses are superior and that plastic thermoses are more effective in maintaining the temperature of cold food than that of hot food.

HOT TEST

Thermos type	7:00 am	12 noon	5:00 pm
Plastic (250 ml)	93°C (199°F)	40°C(104°F)	29°C (84°F)
Glass lined (460 ml)	93°C (199°F)	65°C (149°F)	48°C (118°F)
Steel (470 ml)	93°C (199°F)	78°C (172°F)	70°C (158°F)

COLD TEST

Thermos type	7 am	12 noon	5:00 pm
Plastic (250 ml)	4°C (39°F)	14°C (57°F)	17°C (63°F)
Glass lined (460 ml)	4°C (39°F)	12°C (54°F)	15°C (59 °F)
Steel(470 ml)	4°C (39°F)	8°C (46°F)	9°C (48°F)

Note: For these tests we used small neck thermos bottles which we first cooled or heated as suggested on page 11.

NO CARBONATED BEVERAGES!

They can cause leaks, or worse, blow the cork off the bottle! Furthermore, they are of no nutritional value…

Maintenance

After each use: wash the thermos (do not forget the thread of the neck), the cork and the cup by hand, using hot soapy water and then rinse with hot water. Dry with a soft towel or simply let dry. Store the thermos without the cork or cup to allow for air circulation. Do not immerse the bottle entirely under water or put it in the dishwasher, unless indicated otherwise on the label, as the bottle is not sufficiently waterproof. **Once a week:** Wash with water and a little baking soda to eliminate odors.

Reusable plastic containers

They are round, square, rectangular, oval, or cylindrical, of all sizes and colors! With their tight sealed lid they are practical for carrying cold food and if microwaveable, can be reheated if needed at mealtime. As a bonus, as they are reusable, we save on lunch bags, waxed paper and plastic wrap. It is good for the pocketbook as well as the environment!

THE JUICE BOX

Practical for cold beverages, we can fill and freeze it the night before leaving space to allow for liquid expansion. It will keep the other food cool in the lunch box. **Cost?** Approximately $2.25 to $3.25 for 250 ml and 500 ml respectively.

THE SMALL SQUARE OR RECTANGLE (500 ML OR LESS)

Use for a slice of bread, a piece of cake, salads, cooked chicken, a hard cooked egg or a small portion of pasta. **Cost?** Between $1.50 and $3 based on size.

THE LARGE SQUARE OR RECTANGLE (500 ML TO 1 L)

Perfect for sandwiches (1 or 2 depending on size), a green salad or a cold ready-made meal. **Cost?** From $2 to $5 based on size.

THE SMALL ROUND (500 ML OR LESS)

Ideal for fragile fruit (pear, peach, kiwi, etc.), a fruit salad, pudding, yogurt, muffin, hard cooked egg, soup, salad or a cold ready-made meal. The small round container (118 ml) is ideal for salad dressing, vinaigrette, dip or purée. **Cost?** From $1 to $4 based on size.

THE LARGE ROUND (500 ML TO 1 L)

Ideal for a green salad or a larger ready-made meal. **Cost?** From $2.50 to $4 based on size.

LIGHT MEAL/SANDWICH KEEPER (1.4 L)

It can accommodate a sandwich in its upper part and in its lower part can hold raw veggies, a juice box with a hard cooked egg or a muffin. Dinner is served! **Cost?** Approximately $5.

Fresh idea!

To maintain the freshness of cold foods (soups, sandwiches, salads, ready-made meals) during transportation, place them next to a freezer pack.

And the microwave?

Most of the plastic containers sold in stores today can be used in microwave ovens (check the label to be sure). Before placing the container in the microwave oven, make sure to lift the lid slightly in order to let steam escape. Avoid reheating food with a high content of fat, sugar or tomato (spaghetti sauce, for instance) in order to prevent permanent staining and/or warping of the container. Finally, remember that plastic containers are not for use in a conventional oven, under the broiler or on stove elements.

Empty yogurt, margarine, or cottage cheese containers, etc., are not suitable for reheating food in the microwave. The heat generated by the food (especially foods rich in oil or fat), will cause deterioration of the plastic and will release toxins.

Maintenance

Many reusable plastic containers can go into the dishwasher (check the label). If not, wash them in soapy water and rinse them well in hot water.

Disposable plastic containers

This is a new generation of plastic containers with lids. They are available in various shapes and can be used in the freezer, microwave, and dishwasher. They can be reused several times, but are thinner and therefore less durable than traditional plastic containers.

Cost? Lower than traditional plastic containers, approximately $3.50 for 4 to 6 containers depending on size (between 235 ml and 950 ml).

For whom? They are ideal for children and also for adults who are tired of the loss or damage of more expensive containers.

Complementary accessories

STORAGE WRAPS

Waxed paper, foil wrap, plastic wrap and sandwich bags take less space in the lunch box than plastic containers or thermos bottles, and there is no need to bring them back home. Moreover, food stored in plastic wrap is more readily identifiable by very young children.

These wrapping products are convenient for raw veggies, fresh or dried fruits, nuts, a slice of bread, a muffin, and if you add a freezer pack, you may pack a piece of cheese, a sandwich or any other perishable food. However they are less desirable for soft or fragile food, especially when the lunch box is made of a soft material or contains a thermos, a glass jar or other hard object. Do keep in mind, that after only one use, disposable wraps end up in the garbage.

EMPTY FOOD CONTAINERS

Milk bags, fresh fruit and vegetable bags, spice jars, baby food jars, mini jam jars and small juice and water bottles may be reused once they are washed and dried. However they are not designed for the microwave. Also, be careful with glass containers as they are breakable. As to bread bags, we do not recommend reusing them to wrap food as the ink can deteriorate and contaminate the food. Finally, because brown paper bags are not washable they can only be used once.

UTENSILS

It is usually better to eat with metal rather than plastic cutlery. Of course you could lose them, but who can't find some old mismatched cutlery in their kitchen? Also, for a few dollars it is easy to buy inexpensive metal cutlery in department or dollar stores. However, good quality plastic cutlery can be put through the dishwasher and reused.

THE NAPKIN

A paper napkin can be used to wrap cutlery, fragile fruit, a thermos, or to hide a surprise or even a love note. A washable cloth napkin can be used as well, having the advantage of being reusable.

THE DAMP WIPE

A disposable damp wipe or wet cloth in a plastic bag will do wonders to clean small faces and small sticky hands.

Freezer packs

Freezer packs are designed to keep food cold for a period of 4 to 6 hours. It is not recommended to heat them in the microwave or in any other way unless otherwise indicated. Some freezer packs are sold empty and must be filled with water before use; others contain a reusable non-toxic liquid. Note that once frozen, some foods (juice box, milk box, yogurt, muffin or other freezable food) can be used to cool other items in the lunch box. They save space and do not need to be brought back home.

How to use them? Put them in the freezer the night before for 6 to 8 hours and slip into the lunch box in the morning. For best results, place the previously cooled freezer packs on the food (since cold descends and heat rises).
Cost? $1.40 or more depending on size.

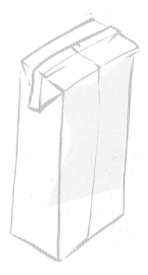

Lunch bags and lunch boxes

There are so many of them! They come in nylon, vinyl, rigid plastic, or in metal, in all sizes, colors and styles! They close with Velcro, zippers or latches. Most have a handle, some have a strap, and others have a strap to attach to a bike or around the waist. Some offer, as a bonus, a mini cooler (for juice box or water bottle) or a freezer pack.

Their cost? Most cost less than $15 and they are worth the investment when one thinks of the savings involved.

Qualities to look for? Of course, it must be attractive. But let's keep in mind that the major reason for a lunch box to exist is to bring your meals to their destination. Thus it is important to ensure that our means of transportation is…

- **durable:** it may have to be submitted to many jolts and all sorts of weather.
- **sufficiently rigid:** nothing worse than a flattened sandwich, a crumbled muffin or fresh fruit reduced to a pulp.
- **the proper size:** not too large so it is not needlessly heavy and cumbersome, nor too small so that it limits the quantity and the variety of food it will contain.
- **sufficiently light:** particularly for the child who will take it to school every morning.
- **easy to clean:** one should have access to every little corner.

THE CLASSIC LUNCH BOX

In hard plastic or in metal, this box is made of two parts superimposed and joined by hinges and latches. The upper section has a handle and is designed to store a thermos bottle. It is a great classic lunch box, of strong construction, durable and easy to clean. This large lunch box is great for those with a good appetite and who like their food hot (it can accommodate 2 thermos bottles). In fact it is the favorite of most blue collar workers.

Its size? 15x22x32 cm (large) and 13x22x28 cm (medium).

What can it contain? (large lunch box) in the upper section: one thermos bottle (460 ml) for beverage and a small plastic round container (235 ml) for milk, sugar or tea bag. **In the lower section:** a thermos bottle (470 ml) for hot food, a sandwich, a bag of raw veggies, a banana, and a small round thermos bottle (235 ml) containing a dessert.

Cost? Approximately $10 for the large lunch box and $8 for the medium box.

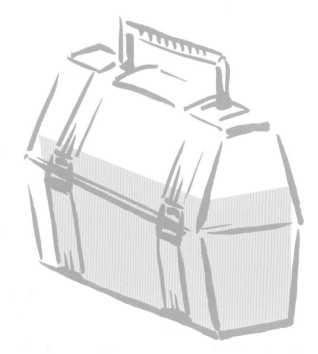

THE BRIEFCASE LUNCHBOX

Perfect for the office! The outside is made of nylon and the inside of vinyl which is easy to clean. It is rectangular, rather thin and hard bodied. Inside, Velcro straps are used to keep the containers from moving. It has space for a canned beverage or juice box but most thermos bottles will not fit. **Its size?** 9x22x29 cm.

What can it contain? A juice box (236 ml), a rectangular plastic container (709 ml) for a salad, a sandwich, a bag of raw veggies and a small yogurt. **Cost?** Approximately $13.

THE SNACK BAG

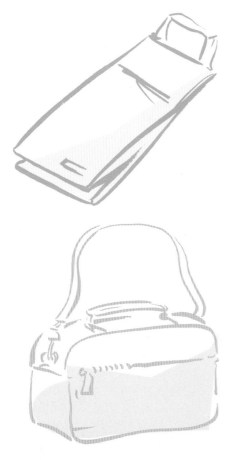

Made of nylon, it has an easy to clean waterproof vinyl lining. Fold it twice and then tighten with the Velcro strap. Although it is not well insulated, it is well suited for a small meal or a snack because of its size.

Its dimensions? 12x18x24 cm. **What can it contain?** A juice box (236 ml), a small round plastic container (235 ml) for a hard cooked egg or a small salad, a small yogurt, a small muffin and a banana. **Cost?** Approximately $5.

THE HARD-BODIED LUNCHBOX

A classic compact lunch box made with a handle and shoulder strap. This lunch box also has a zipper on three sides and the interior has a unique compartment made of rigid plastic that is easy to clean. **Its dimensions?** 11x20x27 cm. **What can it contain?** A thermos bottle (250 ml) for a beverage, a sandwich, a bag of raw veggies, a small round plastic container (235 ml) for a hard cooked egg, or a small salad, a small muffin and a small yogurt. **Cost?** Approximately $13.

THE FOLDABLE SOFT LUNCH BAG

It has an exterior made of nylon, and an easy-to-clean insulated vinyl interior. This bag has a handle and a Velcro closing. It can be flattened to fit in a backpack but is not as desirable for fragile food. **Its size?** 10x18x25 cm. **What can it contain?** A juice box (236 ml), a small round plastic container (235 ml) for a hard cooked egg or a small salad, a small yogurt, a small muffin and a banana. **Cost?** Approximately $7.

THE CHILDREN'S LUNCH BOX

It displays the cartoon characters that our kids love, thus its popularity. Made of rigid plastic, it usually includes a matching plastic thermos bottle. **Its size?** 9x18x22 cm. **What can it contain?** A thermos bottle (250 ml, included with the lunch box) for a beverage, a sandwich, a bag of raw veggies, a banana, and a small muffin. **Cost?** Approximately $10.

THE DOUBLE DECKER BUCKET

It is made of two superimposed and separate compartments. The lower compartment opens on three sides with a zipper. It is easy to clean, made of rigid plastic, and is ideal for a sandwich or other fragile food. This bag has a handle, a Velcro front closing and features good thermal insulation.

Its dimensions? 14x18x27 cm. **What can it contain? In the upper compartment:** a juice box (236 ml), a small yogurt, a small muffin and a banana. **In the lower section:** a sandwich and a bag of raw veggies. **Cost?** Approximately $10.

Upkeep

After each use, thoroughly wash the inside and outside of the lunch box or bag with hot soapy water. Do not forget any corner or fold! Rinse, dry and let it air out all night. Do not put it in the dishwasher.

Chapter 2
The calendar for the week

Have you had enough of the same old ham sandwich prepared quickly on the corner of the table? Tired of last night's leftovers served with the same sauce, day after day? Or tired of the look-alike liquid or solid meal taken on the fly before running off somewhere? Relax! You can prepare a tasty inexpensive lunch, ready to go in your briefcase or backpack 365 days of the year. You need to be a bit organized and self-disciplined. To help, here are a few simple tasks to carry out at different times during the week.

Once a week or less

Be inspired. Leaf through recipe books (like this one) or magazines, and search for attractive menus and recipes. With tabs or a highlighter, mark your good finds or cut them out and place them in an idea file. Meal time with your family is also a good time to solicit suggestions from everyone. Finally, during your weekly visit to the market keep an eye out for fresh produce (new products, fruits, vegetables, and fresh fish) that will enhance your menus.

Plan the menu. Make a list of lunches for the week or for several weeks and rotate them during the course of the year. If you are very methodical, you will note all of the courses from the different meals, from entrée to dessert, taking into account the leftovers from previous meals. If you are not methodical, you may wish to keep track only of the main courses for two or three days of the week. To each his/her own style and way. The important thing is primarily to simplify one's life.

Keep your shelves well stocked. Keeping a variety of foods in the pantry, refrigerator and freezer, both nutritive and quick to prepare (see list on following pages) allows many short cuts when preparing recipes and meals. Even if a number of these time savers (especially those sold in individual servings) cost more, they will help to improvise a last minute lunch from beginning to end, or simply to complete a good home-made meal.

Making a shopping list. When making your weekly grocery shopping list, do not forget to include the food you will need for your lunches.

THE STOCK TO MAINTAIN

Here is a basic list of foods to keep on hand which will supply your lunch box needs and also most of the other meals of the week. With these key items, you will rarely be caught by surprise.

IN THE PANTRY				
Fruits and vegetables	Cereals and grains	Dairy products	Meats and alternatives	Other foods
Fresh fruits (bananas, oranges, apples, cantaloupe)	Various breads (pitas, tortillas, bagels, English muffins, sliced bread)	Milk in Tetra Pak boxes, powdered skim milk and canned evaporated milk	Canned meat and poultry (ham, chicken)	Canned cream soups
Canned fruits (pineapple, peaches, pears, fruit salad, apple sauce, pumpkin puree)	Crackers and biscuits	Ready to eat milk puddings	Canned fish (tuna, salmon, shrimps)	Concentrated broths (vegetable, chicken, beef), dehydrated or in Tetra Pak boxes
Dry fruits (dates, raisins, cranberries, apricots)	Ready to serve cereals (corn flakes) and instant oatmeal		Liquid eggs in Tetra Pak boxes	Soy sauce, mayonnaise, Dijon mustard, ketchup and salsa
Fresh vegetables (potatoes, tomatoes, onions)	Couscous, bulgur, barley, rice (converted white, brown) and pasta (spaghetti, macaroni, penne)		Peanuts, nuts (almonds, pine nuts) and grains (sunflower, pumpkin, sesame)	Oils (olive, canola, sesame)
Canned vegetables (tomatoes — whole and diced, mushrooms, small peas, corn, macedoine, beans)	Cereal bars and biscuits (figs, dates, oatmeal)		Peanut butter	Vinegars (white, red wine, balsamic)
	Bread and muffins (bananas, fruits, nuts)		Canned legumes (red beans, black beans, lentils, green peas)	Herbs and spices (garlic, pepper, parsley, oregano, basil, thyme, tarragon, ginger, cumin, dry mustard)
Fruit or vegetable juice in Tetra Pak boxes	Flour (white, whole wheat)		Canned legume meals (bean salad, beans in tomato sauce, chili)	Sugar, brown sugar, syrup, jam, honey and molasses
Canned tomato paste and sauce	Bread crumbs		Canned soup meals (peas, lentils, minestrone)	Extracts (vanilla, almond)
Dried tomatoes in a container			Canned spaghetti sauce	Corn starch
				Bran and wheat germ
				Unflavored gelatin
				Cocoa

IN THE REFRIGERATOR

Fruits and vegetables	Produits céréaliers	Dairy products	Meats and alternatives	Other foods
Fresh fruits (kiwis, pears, grapes) Fresh vegetables (broccoli, carrots, cauliflower, green and red peppers, celery, green onions, zucchini, mushrooms) Washed and cut raw veggies (grated cabbage, small carrots, and roman lettuce spinach) Juice (vegetables, fruits, tomato, and lemon) Chopped garlic in a jar	Store bought pizza dough	Milk 1% or skim Yogurt 1% or skim (plain, with fruits) Cheese (cheddar, mozzarella, parmesan, cottage, ricotta) sliced and grated Dips for veggies	Fresh and deboned meat and poultry (beef, pork, veal, chicken, turkey, hamburger meat, roasts, cutlets) Cooked meat and poultry (beef, ham, pork, veal, chicken, turkey, roasts, slices) Fresh eggs and hard cooked eggs Vegetarian pâté and chick pea spread (hummus) Store bought vegetarian courses (lasagna, millet pie, leek quiche)	Soft margarine, butter

FREEZER

Fruits and vegetables	Cereals and grains	Meats and alternatives
Frozen fruits (strawberries, raspberries, blueberries) Frozen vegetables (spinach, peas, corn, broccoli, mix of same)	Various breads (pitas, tortillas, bagels, English muffins, sliced bread) Sliced muffins and bread (banana, fruits, nuts) Frozen stuffed pasta (tortellini, ravioli)	Frozen filets of fish Home cooked meals in individual portions Healthy frozen meals (see chapter 6) Home-made spaghetti sauce

Cook on a large scale. For approximately the same amount of time and the same amount of dishes to wash, why not double or triple the recipes to prepare? Soups, lasagnas, Chinese pâtés, stocks: keep the necessary quantity for the meal of the day, and then divide the surplus in individual portions and put them in plastic containers suitable for microwave ovens. Label (name of the meal, preparation date), freeze and there you have a variety of small home-made dishes ready to reheat at your convenience! Another tip: at dinner, prepare a little more meat, vegetables, salad, pasta or rice than necessary. The next day the rice and the beef will become Chinese rice and the pasta and vegetables will become a great base for a delicious cold salad.

A good way to keep the kids busy on a rainy Sunday afternoon is to organize a work crew to make a pile of sandwiches and accompaniments! The idea is to prepare a variety of sandwiches and garnishes by avoiding the ingredients that cannot be frozen (see the list bellow). Then slip the sandwiches in bags or plastic sandwich containers, label (by writing, if appropriate, to whom it belongs) and freeze. With regards to garnishes, put them in ice cube trays and put them in the freezer. When well frozen, transfer the cubes of garnishes in labeled frozen bags. The sandwiches and garnishes can keep 1 or 2 days in the refrigerator and up to 6 weeks in the freezer.

Foods that do not freeze well:

Some fresh fruits (cantaloupe, honey melon, watermelon, grapes)
Some fresh vegetables (tomatoes, celery, cucumber, sprouts, lettuce, radishes)
Home-made yogurt
Some cheeses (brie, camembert, cottage, ricotta, spread of melted cheese, cream cheese)
Milk pudding and jelly
Hard cooked eggs (whole, egg whites)
Mayonnaise, mustard, ketchup, marinades
Preserves

Preparing raw vegetables. The best way to remember to eat your 'veggies' is to have them prepared and close by! A good tip: anticipating your weekly lunches; wash, drain and cut a good quantity of raw vegetables (cherry tomatoes, carrot sticks, broccoli, cauliflower, pepper strips etc.). Distribute them in plastic bags or in a closed plastic container, without water. Place them in the refrigerator. In the morning each one chooses a bag of raw veggies, a sandwich, a beverage and a fruit, and lunch is ready! To save time, you can purchase at the grocery store a variety of bagged (washed and cut) raw vegetables and lettuce ready to eat.

The night before

Prepare all that can be prepared ahead and wrap in sealed packages: cooked meals, sandwiches, (without lettuce or mayonnaise), hard cooked eggs, cheese, nuts, buttered bread, thermos bottles for milk, juice or cold dessert (yogurt, milk pudding, fruit salad, jelly), bags of raw veggies, fresh or dried fruits, salads (shredded lettuces, washed raw vegetables, chicken, ham, fish or cheese cut in pieces), small container of mayonnaise or vinaigrette etc.

Place in the refrigerator. Refrigerating food thoroughly, even the non-perishable ones such as juice boxes, peanut butter sandwiches, muffins and fruits, will allow the content of the lunch box to stay cold longer the following day.

Freeze. Juice or milk boxes and individual yogurts, in particular, can be frozen. When taken out of the freezer the next morning they will act as freezer packs (without taking any space), before thawing and will be thawed and ready to eat or drink at mealtime. And if they have not had time to thaw completely? Crush the contents with your fingers, cut the top of the box and with a spoon enjoy as a sorbet! The kids will ask for more…

FOODS THAT CAN BE FROZEN

	Recommended freezing time
Fruits and vegetables	
Fresh fruits (except cantaloupe, honey melon, watermelon, grapes)	1 year
Fresh vegetables (except tomatoes, celery, cucumber, sprouts, lettuces, radishes)	1 year
Juices (fruits, vegetables)	1 year
Cereals and grains	
Bread (whole, sliced)	3 months
Biscuits, pies and muffins	3 months
Cooked pasta	3 months
Cooked rice	6-8 months
Dairy products	
Milk	6 weeks
Yogurt	1 month
Cheese (except: brie, camembert, cottage, ricotta, melted cheese, spread cream cheese)	6 months
Meats and alternatives	
Fresh meat (hamburger, in cubes, sliced)	3-4 months
Fresh meat (chops, roasts)	4-6 months
Cooked meat (without sauce)	2-3 months
Cooked meat (with sauce)	4 months
Fresh poultry (pieces)	6-9 months
Fresh poultry (whole)	10-12 months
Cooked poultry (without sauce)	1-3 months
Cooked poultry (with sauce)	6 months
Cooked ham (whole, sliced), charcuterie	1-2 months
Fatty fish (salmon, trout, mackerel)	2 months
Lean fish (haddock, arctic char, cod, plaice)	6 months
Prepared cooked meals	3 months
Sandwiches and garnishes	6 weeks
Hard Egg yokes	1 month
Nuts	1 year
Peanut butter	6 months
Tofu	1-2 months
Cooked legumes	3 months
Other foods	
Soups	2-3 months
Soft butter	3 months
Salted butter	1 year
Margarine	3 months

Note: **You cannot re-freeze a food that has been completely thawed without risk of contamination.**

Adapted from The Quebec Ministry of Agriculture and Fisheries. *Fresh is better! Storage limit for perishable foods 1998.*

Take out the frozen cooked meals (except sandwiches which thaw rapidly) from the freezer and place them in the refrigerator. They will then begin to thaw overnight.

In the morning

Finish preparing the salads. Mix the ingredients prepared the night before (lettuce, raw vegetables, hard cooked eggs, chicken, fish, or other ingredients cut in pieces). To maintain the salad's crunch longer, the vinaigrette or mayonnaise can be carried in a separate small container (a small pill box is perfect and its size is large enough) and added only at mealtime.

Fill the thermos bottles.

- **For hot beverages and hot foods.** Preheat the thermos for maximum efficiency. Fill it with boiling water, put the cork in and let it rest for 5 to 10 minutes. In the meantime reheat the cooked food in the microwave oven or on the range (unless you have access to a microwave oven at mealtime) and prepare the hot beverages (coffee, hot chocolate, hot water for tea or herb tea). Empty the thermos of boiling hot water, pour in the hot content and screw the cork and cup on.

- **For cold food and cold beverages.** First cool the thermos by filling it with iced water. Wait for 5 to 10 minutes. Empty the bottle, then fill it with the cold food or beverage (milk, juice, fruit salad, or vegetables, jelly, milk desserts, cooked meal or others), then screw on the cork and cup.

Take the sandwiches, the muffins and the boxes of milk or juice out of the refrigerator.

Take out of the refrigerator the thermos bottles and the foods that were placed in it the night before.

Add lettuce and mayonnaise to the sandwiches.

Put together the lunch box. To avoid ending up with a flattened sandwich or a smashed pear, make sure to place the heaviest or the hardest (the sandwich container or the fruit box for example) at the bottom of the box. Then place the lighter or the most fragile items (such as whole fruits or a sandwich bag) on top.

Add one or two ice packs if frozen milk or juice boxes are not planned in the menu. Place them against the perishable food (milk boxes, sandwiches, salads, cold cooked meals). They will keep the food cold for 4 to 6 hours.

Not to be forgotten: utensils, serviette, plate, tea or herb tea bag, bottle opener, can opener, damp towel, tooth brush or chewing gum, and a love note or a little surprise will do wonders to stimulate one's appetite and digestion…

At work or at school

Avoid sources of heat. Keep lunch away from direct lighting and heaters for instance. As to the perishable foods that are not in lunch boxes or insulated bags with ice packs or thermos bottles (brown paper bag for example) place them in the refrigerator until mealtime.

Reheat in the microwave oven the dishes that are meant to be eaten hot, although they have been carried cold from your house.

Upon your return to the house

Throw out all perishable leftovers: sandwiches, salads, cheese, milk and others. You can, however, keep non-perishable foods that have not been eaten without any problem (such as cup puddings, whole fruits, juice boxes and raisins).

The evening

Clean all equipment used. Wash carefully with a detergent and hot water, rinse thoroughly, turn over to let dry, and then put away. Leave the thermos bottles (without cork or lid) and the lunch box open so they can air out and keep odor-free. For more details on maintenance, consult Chapter 1 on page 9.

THE PERFECT COMBINATION

Here are some suggestions for sandwich fillings, salads, and extras which can be made in a jiffy and which can be modified as you see fit according to your own taste… and to the food's availability! They are ideal to give new life to leftovers such as meat, poultry, rice, raw vegetables, pasta, potatoes, etc. The use here of plain yogurt, no-fat vinaigrette, mustard, skim milk cheese or ultra low fat cream cheese in place of the conventional cheeses, salad sauces, mayonnaises and vinaigrettes will decrease the use of fat significantly.

Sandwich fillings, salads, and extras

- Cream cheese, diced red or green pepper, diced tomato and chopped chives
- Cream cheese, chopped prosciutto, chopped dry tomatoes, chopped black olives and capers
- Cottage cheese, diced apples, diced pears, hulled sunflower seeds and currants
- Plain yogurt, grated cheese, grated apple and chopped nuts
- Plain yogurt with diced carrot, cucumber, and green peppers
- Store bought hummus (chick pea dip), grated carrots and grated zucchini
- Peanut butter, chopped dates and orange juice
- Vegetarian pepperoni in thin slices, grated cheese and soft or hot mustard
- Mashed tofu, diced red onions, grated zucchini and chopped dried tomatoes
- Mashed hard cooked eggs, chopped parsley, chopped stuffed olives, and mayonnaise

- Mashed hard cooked eggs, chopped celery, diced red pepper, alfalfa, chopped onion and mayonnaise
- Chopped cooked chicken, salsa, corn and sour cream
- Chopped cooked chicken, salsa, mango, red pepper and sour cream
- Sliced cooked turkey, pieces of orange, sliced green pepper and plain yogurt
- Slices of roast beef, sweet or sour pickles and cream cheese
- Chopped ham, sweet relish and cream cheese
- Can of flaked tuna, diced red pepper, chopped celery, chopped green onion, and plain yogurt
- Can of flaked tuna, sour pickles, chopped celery and mayonnaise
- Can of flaked salmon, chopped smoked salmon, chopped onion, chopped parsley and lemon juice
- Mashed avocado, chopped shrimp, lemon juice, sliced lettuce and plain yogurt

Salads

When having a salad as a meal, let's not forget a source of protein (cheese, meat, poultry, fish, eggs, vegetarian deli, nuts, legumes, or tofu).

- Tomato quarters, chunks of feta, black olives, slices of onion and oil
- Chayotte, cooked shrimps, sesame seeds, fresh grated ginger, oil and lemon juice
- Spinach, chopped hard cooked eggs, diced tomatoes, chopped onion, alfalfa, chopped prosciutto and plain yogurt
- Romaine lettuce, sliced avocado, sections of grapefruit, diced red pepper and plain yogurt
- Boston lettuce, diced pears, diced red pepper, grated cheese, chopped peanuts, balsamic oil and vinegar
- Canned lentils, diced tomatoes, diced green peppers, grated carrots, chopped parsley, oil and red wine vinegar
- Couscous, diced tomatoes, chopped parsley, chopped green onion, oil and lemon juice
- small cooked pasta (rotini, macaroni, penne), diced tofu, cherry tomatoes cut in half, asparagus in chunks, quartered artichokes and spiced vinaigrette
- Bulgur, canned red beans, chopped onion, diced yellow pepper, diced zucchini, oil and cider vinegar
- Brown rice, canned black beans, corn kernels, diced tomatoes and spiced tomato sauce
- Small cooked pasta (rotini, macaroni, penne), diced ham, chunks of broccoli, grated cheese, sliced mushrooms and mayonnaise
- Potatoes in large morsels, chopped hard cooked eggs, chopped black olives, chopped anchovies, chives and plain yogurt
- Sliced lettuce, diced chicken, green grapes, balls of melon, chopped celery, sliced almonds and plain yogurt
- Sliced Italian tomatoes, meat, poultry, or fish cooked and diced, sliced green pepper, onion rings and Italian vinaigrette
- Grated carrot, chopped parsley, raisins, nuts and lemon vinaigrette

The lunch corner

Unless you want to run around the kitchen in the morning, it is best to keep all necessary equipment in the corner of a cabinet to prepare your lunches: lunch boxes and lunch bags, thermos bottles, plastic wrap, plastic bags and plastic containers, plates, straws, utensils, napkins, bottle opener, can opener, note book and pencil, small bottles for mayonnaise and vinaigrette, and tooth brushes or chewing gum… Include also some non-perishable foods such as milk or juice boxes, bags of nuts and dried fruits, canned fruits and puddings, cereal bars, fruit sauces etc. You can also reserve a section of your refrigerator for the food destined for your lunch boxes: individual yogurts, slices of cheese, hard cooked eggs, salads, etc. Once more, a great way to save precious time.

Chapter 3
Lunch and all the trimmings

P roviding varied lunch menus is not always easy! How do we go about making lunches that meet our nutritional needs while at the same time providing variety and interest? It is as simple as 1, 2, 3!

1. Choose healthy foods

These healthy choices can be found in the four food groups of the Canadian Food Guide*. Here are our winning options, the best of each of these food groups.

FRUITS AND VEGETABLES

Products high in color. Several pigments which give fruits and vegetables their colour are "phytochemicals", called "carotenoids", "flavanoids" or "isoflavones". Most of them act as antioxidants and fight cancer, cardiac diseases and other health problems — a very good reason to fill your shopping basket with a rainbow of colors…
- **Red:** Strawberries, raspberries, cranberries, tomatoes, watermelon, pink grapefruit, guavas
- **Orange:** carrots, sweet potatoes, pumpkin, cantaloupe, oranges
- **Yellow:** corn, squash, grapefruit, lemons
- **Green:** spinach, cabbage, broccoli, brussel sprouts, green peas, leafy green vegetables (kale, mustard leaves, etc.)

- **Blue or purple:** cherries, blueberries, grapes
- **And even white:** garlic, onions, leeks

Whole foods, preferably with skin. They contain more fiber than fruit or vegetable juices. Of course, when one thinks of "fiber" one thinks of "regularity"! But fiber does more than stimulate lazy bowels: it helps prevent or treat a large number of health problems such as diverticulosis, diabetes, cardiac diseases and cancer. Moreover, as fiber provides volume (without the calories!) and slows down the exit of the food from the stomach, it maintains a feeling of fullness for a longer period of time. Great to keep your figure under control.

___
* Consult Health Canada, Canada's Food Guide to Healthy Eating at www.hc-ss.gc.ca

Cantaloupe, strawberries, broccoli and other good sources of vitamin C should be included in every meal, especially those that do not contain meat, poultry, or fish. Vitamin C enhances the solubility of plant based iron, resulting in higher absorption by the body. By consuming less than 75 mg of vitamin C (this is the amount contained in one quarter of a cantaloupe, 1 cup of vegetable juice, 1/2 green pepper or 4 brussel sprouts), one almost doubles the absorption of plant based iron. And by consuming a greater amount (the equivalent of 2 kiwis, a cup of broccoli or cauliflower or a large glass of orange juice or enriched apple juice) one can triple this quantity. The recipes in this book stating "Excellent source of vitamin C", supply 30 mg of this vitamin or more per serving.

CEREALS AND GRAINS

Whole grain products. They contain more minerals (such as magnesium, potassium, and zinc), phytochemicals and fiber than refined products. Some good choices: bread, pasta and bakery products made with 100% whole wheat, whole wheat flakes, uncooked oatmeal, pot barley, crushed wheat and brown rice.

Products (bread, pasta, rice) labeled "enriched" are far superior than refined products (white) because iron and vitamin B have been added to compensate for nutrients lost during processing.

Even if they cannot pretend to equal whole grain products, enriched products are more nutritious than their non-enriched refined cousins.

Fat-reduced baked goods. They help reduce fat, especially bad fat: trans fatty acids and saturated fat often present in store-bought baked goods (muffins, cakes, croissants, doughnuts, Danishes, cookies and crackers).

DAIRY PRODUCTS

Cheeses with 15% fat (mf) or less. Canadians eat on average over 30 g of cheese per day, or the equivalent of a 4 cm cube. For an ordinary cheese with more than 25% mf (cheddar, gouda, brick, ementhal or colby), this represents at least 8 g of fat (as much as 2 pats of butter), of which 5 g is saturated fat (close to 25% of the daily recommended limit).

Milk and yogurt 1% MF or less. Each cup of milk or yogurt at 2% MF produces 3 g of saturated fat, which is substantial. Very low fat varieties have the advantage of having less fat and calories, and just as much protein and calcium.

Peanut butter. Good old peanut butter is an inexpensive source of protein, vitamins and minerals (folic acid, vitamin E, selenium, magnesium, zinc, etc.), antioxidants, fiber and good unsaturated fat. Peanut butter is recommended for long term energy. According to an American study (*American Journal of Clinical Nutrition*, Dec. 1999), without reducing the quantity of fat consumed, changing its quality by consuming more good fat such as peanuts and peanut butter reduces the risk of cardiac diseases by 21%.

Lean meat (without visible fat). Meat contains a type of iron which is particularly well assimilated by the body. It facilitates 2 to 4 times the absorption of plant based iron in a meal. On the other hand, lean meat is a source of saturated fat, which increases the risk of cardiac disease. Red meat is also associated with a higher risk of colon and prostate cancer. The solution? Pick very lean cuts and eat small portions the size of a deck of cards. It is more than enough.

Low fat deli and vegetarian products. Four slices of cooked bacon (80g, raw) contain 12 g of fat, a beef wiener of 60 g contains 16 g of fat, and a typical regular cooked sausage (115 g, raw) contains about 20 g of fat. Roughly one third of these fats are saturated fats. These products are generally full of sodium. Deli chicken and turkey are not necessarily leaner. Our best and safest bets? The low fat meat and vegetarian deli versions (sausages, pepperoni, salami).

Eggs. They are a source of quality protein (one egg contains as much protein as 30 g of cooked meat), vitamins A, D, and B12, riboflavin, folic acid, calcium, iron, zinc… and supply only 75 calories (as much as an apple!), and the equivalent of a teaspoon of fat. Consume 3 or 4 weekly (think cholesterol!). Eggs deserve a place in the diet of a healthy person.

Legumes and tofu. Beans, lentils, peas and tofu help reduce our consumption of meat, saturated fat and cholesterol. They are rich in phytochemicals and fiber (except for tofu) and they are very economical. To get started, begin with store-bought products: chili, beans in tomato sauce, pea soup, or canned minestrone, vegetarian-paté, hummus (chick pea dip), frozen bean burritos and veggie sausages and burgers.

Fish. They contain quality protein, vitamin D (especially sardines, salmon and mackerel), calcium (when bones are eaten), phosphorus, zinc and other nutrients. The fat species, such as mackerel, herring and salmon are an important source of good omega 3 fat. They have an anti-inflammatory effect and stimulate the immune system. Moreover, they help in preventing cancer and cardiac diseases. They lower high blood pressure, help prevent arrhythmia and reduce bad fat in the blood, which in turn reduces the creation of blood clots. So many good reasons to increase your consumption of fish.

2. Put "four" on the table

Each group of the food guide is important. To eat at least one food from each of the four groups at every meal will start you off on the right foot. These foods can be combined in one course (such as a super sandwich with ham, mozzarella, lettuce, bell pepper and tomato). As well, each of the groups can be supplied individually: for example, a hard cooked egg, raw vegetables, a muffin and a cup of milk. It is your choice.

3. Adjusting the right quantity to our needs

The quantity of food a person should consume depends on his or her needs in terms of energy and nutrition. This varies with age, sex, as well as the amount and level of physical activity. This increases as well during pregnancy and breastfeeding. It is obvious that an active teenager will eat considerably more than a kindergarten toddler, and a laborer more than an office worker. For each food group, the Canadian Food Guide suggests a broad selection of food each day for optimal health. The best way to know precisely what quantity is best for your needs is to rely on your appetite! It is your best guide.

NUMBER OF SERVINGS FROM EACH GROUP TO EAT DAILY
AND EXAMPLES OF ONE SERVING

Cereals and grains: 5 to 12 servings daily

Examples of one serving: 1 slice of bread, 1 muffin, 1/2 bagel, pita or English muffin, 125 ml pasta or cooked rice, 30 g ready-made cereal or 175 ml hot cereal.

Fruits and vegetables: 5 to 10 servings daily

Examples of one serving: 1 medium sized fruit or vegetable, 125 ml fresh fruit or vegetables, canned or frozen, or 125 ml juice.

Dairy products: 2 to 4 servings daily

Children (4 to 9 years old): 2 to 3 servings. Youth (10 to 16 years old): 3 to 4 servings. Adults: 2 to 4 servings. Pregnant or breastfeeding women: 3 to 4 servings. Examples of one serving: 250 ml milk, 175 g (3/4 cup) yogurt or 50 g cheese, the equivalent of a piece 3x3x8 cm or 2 slices of processed cheese.

Meats and alternatives: 2 to 3 servings daily

Examples of one serving: 1 to 2 eggs, 30 ml peanut butter, 50 to 100 g meat, poultry or cooked fish, 100 g tofu or 125 to 250 ml cooked legumes.

Why does the number of servings vary for each group?

To take into account the needs of each individual. As early as 4 years of age, most people fill their daily needs by choosing among the quantity of food suggested in the four groups.

For example, an elderly woman or a primary school child could be satisfied with the smaller portion recommended for each group, and a teenager with the higher number. Once again, when quantity is in question, your appetite is the best judge.

Different servings for different people

The quantities in the sample menus below are given only as a guide. Each person is unique even in the way he or she eats! The real number from servings of each food group we must eat daily is therefore very personal.

FOODS		SERVINGS		
Menu 1	Cereals	Fruits	Dairy	Meats
5 year old child				
Fruit juice (box of 200 ml)		1½		
Ham sandwich	2			
(2 slices 25 g)				1
Raw vegetable bag (125 ml)		1		
Fruit yogurt (175 g)			1	
TOTAL	2	2½	1	1
25 year old woman				
Add to the above:				
Cheese				
(1 slice of 25 g)			½	
TOTAL	2	2½	1½	1
16 year old teenager				
Add to the above:				
One 2nd ham-cheese sandwich	2		½	1
One green salad (250 ml)		1		
Or a 2nd bag of raw vegetables				
TOTAL	4	3½	2	2

FOODS	SERVINGS			
Menu 2	**Cereals and Grains**	**Fruits And Vegetables**	**Dairy Products**	**Meats and Alternatives**
5 year old child				
1% skimmed milk (box of 200 ml)			¾	
Hard cooked egg				1
Cherry tomatoes (4-5)		½		
Stick carrots		½		
Whole wheat crackers (4)	1			
Banana bread (1 thin slice)	1			
Clementine (2)		1		
TOTAL	2	2	¾	1
25 year old woman				
Add to the above:				
One 2nd slice of banana bread	1			
TOTAL	3	2	¾	1
16 year old teenager				
Add to the above:				
One peanut butter sandwich (30 ml)	2			1
Cheese (4 cm cube)			1	
Apple sauce (125 ml)		1		
TOTAL	5	3	1¾	2
Menu 3	**Cereals and Grains**	**Fruits And Vegetables**	**Dairy Products**	**Meats and Alternatives**
5 year old child				
Vegetable juice (box of 200 ml)		1½		
Pocket pizza (p. 132)	2	1	½	¼
Chocolate pudding (p. 168)			½	
(1/8 of recipe or 125 ml)				
TOTAL	2	2½	1	¼
25 year old woman				
Add to the above food:				
1 extra chocolate pudding			½	
One bag of nuts (50 ml)				½
TOTAL	2	2½	1½	¾
16 year old teenager				
Add to the above food:				
1 extra pocket pizza	2	1	½	¼
TOTAL	4	3 ½	2	1

Menu tips

Some tips to tune up and rejuvenate your lunches

Include foods from the four food groups with each meal. They each have their respective nutritional values but together they create a high energy mix. For example:

- **Fresh or dried fruits, or juices.** They are full of simple sugars (glucose, fructose, sucrose). These sugars, quickly absorbed and digested, energize us in a few moments. However their action is short lived (less than one hour).
- **Cereals and grains (bread, muffins, cereals, rice, pasta) and legumes.** Their complex sugars which are digested in 1 to 3 hours, are gradually absorbed into the blood stream. They therefore replace simple sugars for long-term energy. And as these foods are low in fat, they are easily digested.
- **Dairy products, meats and alternatives (milk, cheese, meat, eggs, peanut butter, nuts, legumes, tofu).** Thanks to their protein, fat, and (for the peanuts, nuts and legumes) their fiber, these foods contribute to the feeling of being full, and slow down the absorption of glucose in the blood creating energy that lasts and lasts…

Include enough protein with each meal. They are essential to avoid feeling exhausted by midday! This requires planning at least one serving of meat or alternative per meal (see size of serving on p. 30). This is the equivalent of 15 to 20 g of protein. Note: soups, salads and other recipes in this book which bear the word 'main course' supply at least 15 g of protein per serving and consequently can constitute the main ingredient of the meal.

Avoid fat or very salty foods. Especially before intellectual or physical effort.

- **Fatty foods** (deli, meats and high fat cheeses, deep fried food, pastries, chocolate, crackers, etc.): they digest in 5 to 7 hours. Consequently, blood remains in the stomach, where it is essential to digestion, rather than in the brain or muscles!
- **Salty foods** (crackers, soups, sauces, pizzas, frozen dinners, bacon, sausages, ham and other store-bought processed foods): they thicken the blood, dehydrate our cells and force the kidneys to eliminate excess salt.

Avoid alcohol. By numbing the brain, it weakens our faculties (judgment, self control and attention), slows down our reflexes, and interferes with coordination. It also dehydrates our body by forcing our kidneys to eliminate fluids. Before a sporting or mental event, alcohol can contribute to a loss of control.

Limit the use of coffee. Caffeine in coffee leaches calcium from the bones which is then eliminated in the urine. It can reduce fertility and increase the risk of miscarriage. At night it can delay or disturb one's sleep which is so important to body cell repair. It is best then to drink no more than 2 to 3 cups of coffee a day. And if our intestines have a tendency to be uptight before a presentation, an exam, or other stressful activity, it is best to abstain as caffeine stimulates the intestines!

Drink tea, preferably between meals. Tea is rich in flavonoids, substances that act as antioxidants. It also contains caffeine (commonly called 'tannin') but 2 or 3 times less than coffee, so that one can easily drink 6 to 8 cups (depending on the type of tea and steeping time) per day. Avoid drinking tea during meals. Its tannin traps the iron and stops it from being absorbed. Just one cup of tea can reduce the iron absorption rate by two thirds. It is better to drink tea at least 2 hours after a meal or plan a good source of vitamin C at mealtime to neutralize the effect of tannin.

Enjoy good unsaturated fat. Some fats supply fatty acids essential to the body, others play an important role in the protection against cardiovascular disease. Unsaturated fat is found especially in fatty fish, nuts and grains, vegetable oils (canola, olive, sunflower, soy) and soft non-hydrogenated margarine made from these oils.

Create variety in your menus. Even your favorite foods lose some of their attractiveness when they appear too often on the menu. However, no food is perfect. Even within a group of given foods, each one has strengths and weaknesses. Diversify and benefit from the best each food has to offer, supplying your body's daily requirements.

Appeal to your senses. Seeing, tasting, smelling, touching and even listening are all part of the pleasure of eating. One only has to imagine a meal composed of a white fish sauce with potatoes, cauliflower, vanilla pudding and a glass of milk… and furthermore, the sight, smell, taste and even the thought of food stimulates digestion. These senses increase the secretion of saliva (referred to as 'mouthwatering'), and stomach fluids and helps move food through the digestive system. Another interesting fact: the stimulation of our senses by an attractive meal causes hormonal changes which result in burning from 30 to 40 more calories. At a rate of 3 meals per day for a year, the total would be about 36,500 calories, the equivalent of 4 kilos of fat!

Cut down on very sweet desserts. Most of the very sweet foods (pastries, chocolate, ice cream, cookies) contain a lot of fat (particularly bad trans fat and saturated fat) and are very caloric but not very nutritious. Eating these foods replace the digestive space for healthier foods. And for some sensitive people (they are called 'insulin resistant' because the insulin created by their pancreas is not sufficient to make blood sugar penetrate the inside of the cells, where it is burnt as energy or stored as fuel) sugar increases the risk of cardiac disease by raising triglycerides (a type of fat).

Avoid pigging out. It takes longer and it is harder to digest a big meal, particularly in stressful daily activities. In fact, in a situation when anxiety prevails (exams, presentations, urgent work to finish), the reaction of the body is to force the blood to flee the digestive system (where it is necessary for digestion and absorption) to the benefit of the extremities. A light meal facilitates digestion and has the advantage of being easily integrated in a busy schedule.

The favorite treats

What are the foods that the kids and grown ups are crazy about? To find out we have asked students (kindergarten and Grade 6) and their parents what were their favorite dishes, desserts, fruits, vegetables, snacks, and preferred sandwiches. Here are their choices in the top 5 for each of the questions asked.

KINDERGARTEN (5-6 YEARS OLD)

Main course	Dessert	Fruit	Vegetable	Snack	Sandwich
Spaghetti	Chocolate cake	Apple	Carrot	Cereal bar	Ham*
Shephard's Pie	Ice cream	Strawberries	Cucumber	Chocolate cookie	Cheese
Macaroni and cheese	Chocolate pudding	Banana	Pepper	Muffin	Chicken
Pizza	Yogurt	Pear	Cauliflower	Apple	Eggs
Sausages	Chocolate cookies	Raisins	Broccoli	Marshmallow squares	Tuna

*with or without cheese
(66 respondents)

6TH GRADE (11-12 YEARS OLD)

Main course	Dessert	Fruit	Vegetable	Snack	Sandwich
Pizza	Ice cream	Peach	Cucumber	Cookies	Chicken
Spaghetti	Chocolate cake	Mango	Carrot	Fruit	Ham*
Lasagna	Sugar tart	Strawberries	Tomato	Muffin	Tomato
Macaroni	Doughnut	Watermelon	Pepper	Yogurt	Peanut butter
Beef stock fondue	Popsicles	Apple	Broccoli	Popsicles	Turkey

*with or without cheese
(48 respondents)

PARENTS

Main course	Dessert	Fruit	Vegetable	Snack	Sandwich
Red meat	Pastries	Apple	Asparagus	Fruit	Ham*
Pasta	Chocolate dessert	Mango	Carrot	Cheese	Chicken
Fish	Chocolate cake	Orange	Broccoli	Yogurt	Tomato
Spaghetti	Fruit tart	Peach	Tomato	Nuts	Eggs
Sushi	Fruit	Raspberries	Salad	Muffin	Tuna

*with or without cheese
(105 respondents)

Chapter 4
Precautions to take

Outsmart bacteria

Like us, bacteria appreciate a good meal. In fact they love food that is damp, not too acidic, and very rich in protein like meat, poultry, fish, eggs and dairy products. They are insatiable! Did you know that at a temperature between 35°C and 45°C (95°F to 113°F), their number can double every 15 minutes? At this rate, 100 bacteria can produce more than one million new bacteria in only 3 hours.

Several thousand cases of food poisoning are registered yearly in Canada. But Health Canada estimates that the actual number of cases is closer to 2,000,000. Besides, if you have ever suffered from nausea, vomiting, abdominal cramps and diarrhea, you may have been the victim of food poisoning without knowing it. Most case are mild and do not last more than a few days. However, the consequences can be more serious, especially for elderly people, children, pregnant women or anyone whose immune system has been weakened by cancer or AIDS. There is no point in taking unnecessary risks, especially when, in almost all cases, food poisoning is avoidable.

SAFE FOODS

The following foods do not provide an ideal environment for bacteria, so they can be left at room temperature without the need of thermoses or ice packs. However be careful, as safe foods do not stay that way forever. And when a safe food is mixed with a risky one (see list on following page) the result becomes automatically a risk food.

Fruits and vegetables	Cereals and grains	Dairy products
Fruits, raw, cooked or dried	Ready-to-serve cereals (without milk)	Milk and milk beverages in Tetra Pak* boxes
Raw vegetables	Cereal bars and cookies	Hard cheeses (cheddar, mozzarella,
Fruit or vegetable juices in Tetra Pak* boxes	Muffins and cakes	brick or others)
	Bread, crackers and biscuits	Store-bought puddings
		(sold at room temperature)

Meat and alternatives	Other foods	Other foods (2)
Peanuts, nuts and grains	Oil and vinegar	All foods that are canned, in jars
Peanut butter	Butter and margarine	or in Tetra Pak* boxes
Canned* chicken, ham, fish and other meats	Pickles, mustard, ketchup and relish	
Dry sausages (salami, pepperoni and others)	Jams, honey, syrup, candies and sugar	
	Coffee, tea and herb tea	*Unopened

RISKY FOODS

They must be treated with extreme care to avoid bacterial contamination. These foods, even cooked, should never be left at room temperature more than two consecutive hours or for more than four hours in total, between the time of purchase and consumption — unless of course you have access to the proper equipment (thermoses or ice packs).

Fruits and vegetables	Cereals and grains	Dairy products	Meat and alternatives	Other food
Cooked Vegetables*	Cooked cereals, pasta and rice	Milk*, milk beverages* and cream	Cooked legumes*	Mayonnaise
Fruit and vegetable juice (sold refrigerated)		Yogurt	Meats, poultry and raw or cooked fish*	
		Puddings (home made or refrigerated store bought)	Processed meats (meat patés, ham, bologna etc.)*	
* Except those that are canned, in jars or in Tetra Pak boxes (unopened).		Fresh cheeses (cottage, quark or ricotta)	Raw or cooked eggs*	
			Tofu	

Infamous mayonnaise!

According to some, no food is more fearsome. In reality, mayonnaise is rather acidic (because of the vinegar), and bacteria hates acidity. In fact, it is the combination of mayonnaise with chicken, eggs, fish or other protein foods that creates the risk. These foods reduce the acidity of the mix and add protein to bacteria's menu, a great boost to bacterial growth. The solution? Keep the dish containing mayonnaise in a thermos bottle or use an ice pack in the lunch box.

The choice of foods

- If we use a lunch box with thermoses or ice packs for an outdoor meal, and an icebox or backpack with freezer packs, there is no limit to the type of food we can bring with us. Even perishable food such as egg sandwiches, potato salad, roasted chicken, or custard can be taken, because the equipment will maintain the food at the appropriate temperature.

- If we use a backpack, a brown paper bag, a wicker basket or any other non-insulated wrap, it is preferable to bring safe foods (peanut butter sandwich, raw vegetables, cubes of cheddar, muffin, nuts, fresh fruits, or juice in Tetra Paks), which can be exposed without danger to the local temperature for several hours. If we choose risky foods (those that are milk based, yogurt, eggs, poultry, etc.) they must be kept in the refrigerator until mealtime, or consumed within 2 hours after taking them out of the refrigerator.

Take good care

From the grocery store to your dinner plate the following precautions will help you reduce the risks of contamination.

When purchasing

Check the food. Note the 'best before' expiry dates printed on the bread, juice, milk, yogurt, cheese, eggs, deli items and meat labels. Avoid buying cracked eggs or damaged cans or wrap; their contents could have been contaminated.

Make sure that they are well packaged. Ask that frozen foods and fresh meats be packed together to help maintain their cold temperature.

When storing

Put the refrigerated and frozen food away quickly. Remember that room temperature is particularly suitable to the reproduction of bacteria. Refrigeration slows down their multiplication and freezing puts them to sleep.

Place raw meats and poultry on plates. This will keep their juices from leaking onto and contaminating other foods, especially those that are ready-made or cooked (hard cooked eggs, cooked meats or salads, desserts etc.).

Wrap the food. Cover it with plastic wrap or a lid, or place it in sealed containers. This way we avoid having it being contaminated by other foods. The reverse is also appropriate so that raw meats and poultry, for example, do not drip on other foods and contaminate them.

Avoid leaving perishable food at room temperature needlessly. As a general rule, they should never be left at room temperature for more than 2 consecutive hours or for more than 4 hours all together. These foods should be taken out of the refrigerator only at the time of serving and returned to the refrigerator immediately after.

Keep the temperature of the refrigerator at a maximum of 4°C (40 °F) and that of the freezer at -18°C (0°F). It is a good idea to keep a thermometer in the fridge and freezer and to check the temperature from time to time!

Cook or freeze (if not pre-frozen) poultry, roasts and raw steaks within 3 days following purchase, and hamburger meat and raw giblets within 24 hours. If a food has been completely thawed it must be cooked before refreezing.

Use the food within the recommended time limits (see "Foods that can be frozen" p. 23). However, note that once the container is open, the expiry date labeled on some foods (bread, milk, yogurt, juice, cheese, etc.) is no longer valid and the food generally must be refrigerated and consumed within a few days.

Wash fruits and vegetables well. This will eliminate dirt and part of the bacteria as well as pesticide residues.

Defrost frozen food slowly. Place it in the refrigerator, or in cold water (by sealing the food in a plastic bag and changing the water occasionally so it remains cold), or in the microwave oven by following the manufacturer's directions. Thawing at room temperature (on the counter) is not advised, unless the food is insulated by wrapping in towels or in layers of brown wrapping paper. The idea is to keep the food's surface cool until its center is completely thawed.

Wash your hands as often as necessary. This means: before starting to work, after having handled raw foods (i.e. eggs, meat or poultry), after blowing your nose, after sneezing, and after using the washroom...and don't forget the soap!

Cook hamburger meat and poultry well. As they are more sensitive to contamination, cook them at 160°C (325°F) or more to allow for a quick increase of the internal temperature of the food. Cooking is complete when they do not show any sign of pink coloration.

Refrigerate food as soon as possible after it is cooked. It is best to refrigerate food when it is lukewarm rather than waiting until it is completely cold (dividing it into several small containers speeds up the process).

Wash cutting board, utensils, and hands between each food preparation. Make sure to prepare cooked foods (meat, poultry, and eggs) or ready-made food (salad, raw vegetables, bread) before raw foods to avoid their possible contamination.

Clean your kitchen. Once the food preparation is finished, wash utensils, dishes, cutting board and kitchen counters with bleach diluted in water (5 ml bleach for 750 ml water). This will kill surface bacteria.

Refrigerate all lunch box foods the night before. Non-perishables (muffins, fresh fruits, juice boxes and others) can be included; this will keep the content of the lunch box cool and fresh longer the next day.

Avoid leaving food at room temperature when possible. Keep cold food cold, and hot food hot.

- **For cold dishes (salads, sandwiches, yogurt, milk, etc.):** use a thermos that has been pre-cooled (see "For maximum efficiency" p.11) or use a waterproof plastic container to be kept refrigerated, or leave in the lunch box and put a freezer pack on top.
- **For hot dishes (cooked meals, soups, pasta)** use a thermos bottle that has been previously scalded (see "For maximum efficiency" p.11); or, if the dish is to be reheated at mealtime, place it in a waterproof plastic container kept cold with an ice pack.

Leave the lunch box in a cool or cold place. Avoid placing in direct sunlight (a window ledge for example), or close to heaters and heat sources.

Sort and throw out all perishable leftover food, and if it has been handled, non-perishable food as well. Non-perishable food that is well wrapped or boxed (i.e. juice box, bag of nuts or raisin box), can be re-used. Never trust your eyes, nose or taste buds to assess if a food is still safe to eat. Contaminated food usually cannot be recognized (i.e. odor, appearance or a particular taste).

Clean all equipment. Wash lunch box, thermoses, plastic containers and utensils after each use. (For more details, see chapter "Let's get started!" p. 9.)

Tetra Paks – Practical!

These rectangular cardboard "drink boxes" containing juice, milk or other beverages do not need any refrigeration; they do not break and can be stacked easily to save space in the cupboard or the lunch box. Once frozen, they can even be used as ice packs to keep food cold. As a bonus they are 100% recyclable and do not need to be brought back home!

Anticipate food allergies

Food allergies have nothing to do with parental anxiety or being capricious: they are real, often debilitating and sometimes deadly. To avoid unnecessary risk, here is a list of precautions to consider for children (allergic or not) who go to kindergarten or primary school each day.

- From 1% to 2% of the population suffers from food allergies. Among young children this rate grows to about 5% and is increasing dramatically.
- Peanuts, nuts, sesame, fish, seafood, wheat, soy, cow milk, and eggs represent 90% of serious allergies. But one can be allergic to almost anything: rice, mustard, celery, parsley, banana, kiwi…
- Allergy to peanuts is one of the most common forms of allergy and is by far the main cause of anaphylactic shock, a serious allergic reaction, which can result in death without rapid intervention. Peanuts alone are responsible for more than 50% of the deaths associated with food allergies!
- Poorly washed hands may carry traces of allergens that can be transferred to the mouth, causing an allergic reaction. An allergic reaction could also occur if a person consumes a food that has been in contact with other food to which he or she is allergic.

HOW TO PREVENT?

One cannot expect a primary school child to take full responsibility for food allergies. It is the responsibility of all (parents, teachers, friends, and neighbors) to supervise and encourage the efforts of the child who is learning. Here are some suggestions.

At home

Do not include peanuts, peanut butter or foods that contain them in the lunch box as there may be a child in the nursery or at school who has a severe peanut* allergy. A cheese sandwich, meat spread or hummus (chick pea spread) is a healthy and economical alternative to the traditional peanut butter sandwich. To detect foods that contain peanuts, read thoroughly the list of ingredients on the label, particularly on snack bars, pastries and cookies. Do not forget that many terms can indicate the presence of peanuts (groundnuts): peanuts, artificially flavored peanuts (mandelonas – peanuts that have been deflavored, usually soaked in almond flavoring or other flavoring to give them another 'assumed' life), artificial nuts, ground nuts or mixed nuts. Be careful even with well-known brands as manufacturers sometimes modify their recipes!

Foods that mention: "may contain traces of peanuts" on the packaging present little risk and can be given to a child who is not allergic. Plan for snacks that the majority of children (allergic or not) can eat, such as fruits or vegetables. Their health will profit by it!

At mealtime

At the nursery, insist that food to be heated for allergic children go in the microwave first. An alternative is to use microwave-proof plastic containers with an anti-splash opening in order to prevent contamination of the contents by traces of other foods possibly present in the microwave. Encourage children not to share food, utensils or containers with a classroom friend. For a person who is allergic, a fork, a plate, or a container that has been in contact with the problem food can be dangerous.

---

* A recommendation of la Societe canadienne d'allergie et d'immunologie clinique (the Canadian Society of Allergy and Immunology Clinic), de l'Association des allergologues et immunologues du Québec (Quebec Association for Food Allergies), and the Association of Canadian School Board Advisory.

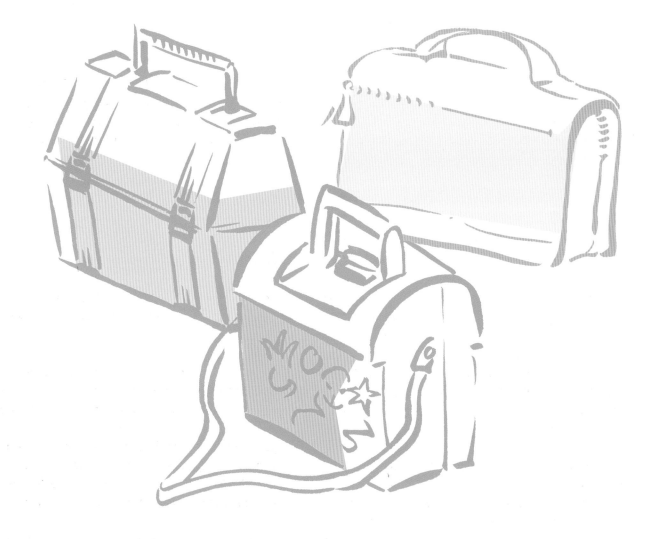

Chapter 5
No time to eat?

Today, men and women do not have enough time to prepare their meals. Worse, they do not have enough time to eat! Dinner hour is being reduced due to time spent on work, family and social obligations. As a result, many neglect their lunch or they skip it all together! It is too bad because taking the time to eat at midday produces benefits which can be measured positively in many ways other than calories and nutrients.

WHY EAT AT LUNCH TIME?

The time one allows oneself to eat lunch enriches both body and mind. It is beneficial in many ways.

1. **To maintain health.** People who skip lunch have greater difficulty obtaining all of their daily nutritional needs from the other meals of the day. It is not surprising that these people have to do just as much with less. A meal does not only supply nutrients: it gives pleasure, it gives the opportunity to socialize, it also gives you something else to think about and allows you to relax and enjoy; in short, it also brings a good dose of mental energy.

2. **To avoid needless stress.** After about 5 hours without eating, blood glucose (the preferred fuel of the brain and muscles) is at its lowest level and can no longer supply the cells' needs. In order to maintain a supply of energy, the body must rally its reserves under the action of emergency hormones such as adrenalin. The body sends alarm signals (headaches, nausea, irritability, lack of concentration). By eating regularly, one maintains a blood glucose level sufficient enough to supply the body's needs.

3. **To be in top form.** To spend a morning studying, working, cleaning the house or doing the shopping, drains one's energy. When you "forget" to eat, fatigue sets in and productivity goes down. By giving yourself a moment to enjoy your lunch on a park bench and then doing a bit of shopping, taking a gentle walk or doing some exercise, you recharge physically and mentally. Sometimes taking a break for a few moments is enough to obtain hours of increased productivity.

4. **To keep your figure.** You do not manage your weight by skipping a meal. The savings in calories are often cancelled

when you compensate by eating more later on in the day. It is easier to control your appetite and calories when you eat regularly. It is easier to resist the second helping of dessert and the sweet at coffee break. Moreover, the body burns calories more efficiently.

HOW TO REACH IT?

There are strategies to meet the needs of our body. It is up to us to choose one that is suitable.

1. **Make the meal a priority.** Write it down on your agenda as a compulsory activity, which it should be. When the temptation comes to ignore it, remember that one always finds the time to do what one really wants to do!

2. **Choose "instant food".** Some choices that do not require preparation, cooking, or reheating: juices, salad, cold chicken, hard cooked egg, cheese, sandwich, cooked meals already hot (carried in a thermos), or yogurt. Just open and eat!

3. **Plan on "combos".** Combine foods belonging to more than one group. Some examples: a mix of muesli and yogurt, minestrone soup, rice salad with lentils, a slice of pizza, a turkey sandwich with gruyere cheese, alfalfa, and tomato, macaroni with tomato au gratin, or even an occasional liquid meal (for more information go to chapter 6). There are many nutritious meals which can be eaten in one's hand when every minute counts!

4. **Keep a supply of portable** "just-in-case" foods. These individual packages travel well and can be slipped into a briefcase, purse or glove compartment of the car when you need to eat on the run, with no fuss and no muss. To anticipate unknown situations, you can leave some in the desk drawer at the office or in the locker at school, or if you have access to it, in the refrigerator at the cafeteria. One tip: remember to keep some utensils, a plate, napkins and a can opener handy! (See p. 45)

5. **Eat piecemeal.** In some circumstances, this is the only way to eat. A work deadline? An outing, a meeting, or a last minute appointment? Short of gulping down your lunch you can eat a small amount at a time, especially if the food is in individual portions.

AND WHAT IF WE EXERCISE AT LUNCH HOUR?

Here are some tips on eating properly when planning to jog, walk, play tennis, swim, do aerobics or strength training at lunch time.

In the afternoon preceding the exercise
Eat a solid breakfast including food from at least 3 of the 4 food groups.
Drink regularly. Water is the preferred beverage, as it hydrates the body and is quickly absorbed by the digestive system. Fruit juices, oranges, and sport beverages (especially those that have a maximum of 10% sugar because they are assimilated faster) are also valid options, particularly during sustained effort (more than 2 hours). As well as hydrating the body, they supply the fuel-sugars of rapid absorption and replace the minerals lost in perspiration.

EXAMPLES OF PORTABLE "JUST-IN-CASE" FOODS

Fruits and vegetables	Cereals and grains	Dairy products	Meats and alternatives	Other foods
Fresh fruit or fruit cups Fruit in baby jars Juice in Tetra Pak boxes Dried fruit bags Raw vegetable bags	Dry cereals (Cheerios type), Oat bran, Wheat flakes, Shreddies etc.) in small boxes or packaged in small sealed containers Crackers or whole grain bagels Cereal bars and cookies (figs, dates, oatmeal) Muffins and breads (Bananas, fruits, nuts)	Milk box (P) Sliced or string cheese (P) Vegetable mini-dip (store bought) (P) Individual yogurts in container or tube (P) Drinking yogurts (P) Puddings (milk, rice, tapioca) in cups	Peanut butter in individual portions Hard cooked eggs (in their shell) (P) Bags of nuts or grains Tuna, salmon or other fish in small cans	Milks (soy, rice) in Tetra Pak boxes

The items followed by a "P" are more perishable and should not be kept at room temperature for more than 2 consecutive hours. For more details on food preservation, see Chapter 4.

Avoid alcohol. It dulls the brain and dehydrates the body, which may result in fainting!

One hour before exercise

Eat a snack based on carbohydrates: i.e., a banana with yogurt, dried fruits and some nuts, fruit juice and a muffin, cereal with milk, a sandwich and a glass of milk, or soup with a slice of bread. Drink up to 500 ml of liquid. The remaining time before the exercise will allow appropriate hydration and elimination of any excess water. Juices and beverages designed for athletes are preferred because the sugars in these drinks provide an appropriate reserve of glycogen.

Just before exercise

Do not eat. Most of the blood will remain available to the arms and legs rather than being routed to the stomach where it is essential for digestion. However, hydration can be maintained by drinking juices and sport beverages.

During exercise

It is not usually necessary to eat.
If the activity lasts less than one hour: drink a small quantity of fresh water at regular intervals, about 4 to 5 sips of 200 to 250 ml every 15 to 20 minutes. This will compensate for the loss of water. The more one sweats the more important this is.
If the activity lasts more than one hour: fruit juices or sport beverages will help maintain performance.

After exercise

Drink immediately to replenish water in the body. If exercise lasts more than an hour, fruit juices and other sugar beverages will replenish water reserves and energy. For a greater impact, one should drink sugared beverages 15 to 30 minutes after exercising. Eat another more substantial snack or a meal, and continue to hydrate.

Chapter 6

Fast-food restaurants, frozen dinners and dinner substitutes

No time or interest to make your lunch? There are always fast-food restaurants, frozen dinners and substitute dinners. However, how valid are these options? The daily needs of an adult woman from 25 to 49 years of age are, on average, 1900 calories and, at most, 65 g of fat (of which 21 g are saturated fat) are needed. For a man in the same age group, around 2700 calories and 90 g of fat (of which 30 g are saturated fat). Sodium should be limited to 2500 g or less for both men and women.

Fast-food restaurants

One suspected it: fast-food restaurants are traps for sodium, calories and fat, and in particular saturated fat and trans fat, those very fats that clog your arteries. Managing to have a 'decent' fast-food meal is not a simple task.

NUMBERS...

Note: French fries and other fried foods available in fast-food outlets are also sources of trans fat which are at least as bad for your arteries as the saturated fat found in hamburgers or cheese. Unfortunately the information given by the fast food chains does not usually include much information about these bad fats.

At Burger King, a Whopper with cheese contains 730 calories, 46 g of fat (the equivalent of 9 tsp. of butter) 16 g of saturated fat and 1300 mg of sodium. It is often eaten with the usual french fries (400 calories, 20 g of fat, 5 g of saturated fat, 240 g of sodium), and mini salt shaker (390 mg of sodium). Add to that, a cinnamon Danish (390 calories,

13 g of fat, 10 g of saturated fat, 305 mg of sodium) and pop (152 calories) and we have 1700 calories and our complete fat and sodium allowance for the day.

Chicken burgers, do they have less fat? At McDonald's, a chicken sandwich (533 calories, 29 g of fat) produces as many calories and fat as a quarter pounder with cheese (534 calories, 30 g of fat) or the Big Mac (541 calories, 30 g of fat).

So a McWrap then? OK, it produces less than 10 g of fat. But it contains as much sodium as an individual pizza, or more than 1000 mg sodium. No, nothing is ever perfect…

The fries, a 'side dish'? A large serving of McDonald's fries (519 calories, 24 g of fat, 12 g of saturated fat) has as much calories, fat and saturated fat as a Big Mac (541 calories, 30 g fat, 10 g of saturated fat).

A turnover with this? Even 'oven cooked' (280 calories, 14 g of fat, 4 g of saturated fat), a fruit turnover of the McDonald type contains roughly the same amount of calories, fat and saturated fat as a cheeseburger (311 calories, 14 g of fat, 6 g of saturated fat).

A muffin then? At Burger King, a carrot muffin (without adding any butter!) contains 430 calories and 20 g of fat. An apple tart contains 'only' 310 calories and 15 g of fat. A store-bought muffin really takes the cake! Most are made from white flour and contain between 350 and 450 calories, from 10 to 20 g (2 to 4 tsp.) of fat and from 25 to 35 g (6 to 9 tsp.) of sugar.

… AND SOLUTIONS!

To avoid our next "gorging" of fast food driving us straight to the hospital coronary unit, here are some healthy tips.

As side dishes
Instead of: cream soup, french fries, fried onion rings, or creamy salads (Caesar, potato, cabbage or macaroni salad)
Choose: green salad with light vinaigrette (limit the croutons, bacon bits and full fat cheese), traditional cabbage salad, or vegetable soup with peas and onions.

For the sandwiches

BREAD
Instead of: croissants
Choose: any other variety of bread! The choice is huge and most are low in fat.

THE FILLINGS
Instead of: a quarter pounder hamburger, meats from the deli (ham, smoked meat, pressed turkey or chicken) or chicken, tuna or egg salad
Choose: a small hamburger patty (60 g), roast beef, turkey or chicken breast without skin, canned salmon or tuna, vegetarian pâté or hummus.

CONDIMENTS
Instead of: full fat cheese, butter, or mayonnaise
Choose: non-hydrogenated soft margarine, low fat mayonnaise or salad dressing, mustard, ketchup, relish, salsa, fat-free cheese, pickles or bell peppers.

For dessert

Instead of: ice cream, milk shake, pie, brownie, cheese cake, giant muffin, turnover (even 'oven baked'!) or chocolate chip cookies

Choose: fruit salad, sorbet, milk ice cream, fat-free yogurt, small muffin or a larger low fat one.

"MAY I TAKE YOUR ORDER?"

Here are two typical fast food meals. You judge the difference.

Regular Mac	Super Mac
Breadcrumbed chicken burger	**Roasted chicken burger**
(533 cal, 29 g MF, 6 g sat. fat)	(310 cal, 8 g MF, 2 g sat. fat)
Fries (medium serving)	**Green salad, light vinaigrette (30ml)**
(400 cal, 19 g MF, 9 g sat. fat)	(70 cal, 6 g MF, 1 g sat. fat)
Turnover 'oven-baked'	**iced milk cone**
(280 cal, 14 g MF, 4 g sat. fat)	(152 cal, 5 g MF, 3 g sat. fat)
Pop (medium size)	**Apple juice (180 ml)**
(215 cal, 0 g MF, 0 g sat. fat)	(76 cal, 0 g MF, 0 g sat. fat)

The result

Regular Mac Meal: 1428 calories, 62 g fat and 19 g saturated fat. It does not include any dairy products, and if we exclude the french fries, the bit of lettuce in the hamburger, and the 'jam' of the turnover, we have neither fruit nor vegetable in the meal.

Super Mac Meal: 608 calories, 19 g fat, 6 g saturated fat. It includes each of the four food groups.

Frozen dinners

Let's be honest: manufacturers of frozen dinners have been creative in their menus since the beginning of TV dinners shortly after the advent of television in 1954. They have since cut down in both fat and salt content (even though there is still a way to go!). Unfortunately, they have also cut down on the amount of food.

SOME NUMBERS...

Calories: Most "lean" or "light" frozen dinners have from 250 to 350 calories. This is the same as a muffin or a yogurt or regular ice cream. This is fine for a snack rather than for a main course which easily contains 500 calories or more.

Vegetables. Rare are the frozen dinners that have more than a 'small' half a cup of vegetables (the equivalent of one of the 5 to 10 recommended daily servings of fruits and vegetables). The popular *Stouffer's 'Lean Cuisine'* orange chicken recipe contains one tablespoon each of carrots and broccoli! Wow!

Dairy products. Except for the meals that include cheese (macaroni and cheese, lasagna, pizza etc.), few include dairy products, which are good sources of calcium.

Fat. Even if the amount of fat indicated on the label of the packaging seems low, it can be misleading when you count the full amount of calories in the meal (all you need to do is calculate the amount of fat per 100 calories). For example, with its 11 g of fat for 299 calories, the Savarin turkey slices are not any leaner than *Michelina's 'Lifestyle'* macaroni and cheese, which contains 14 g of fat for 374 calories.

Sodium. *Piazza Tomasso's* lasagna with meat sauce has 1250 mg of sodium (half of the recommended amount of sodium intake for the whole day) and only 409 calories. Again, it is by comparing the amount of sodium and calories that we can best evaluate the amount of sodium in a meal. It is too bad that the amount of sodium is rarely indicated on the packaging!

... AND THE SOLUTIONS ARE!

Pick the frozen dinners which contain:
- A maximum of 3 g of fat, of which 1 g is saturated fat, per 100 calories (which means, for a meal of 300 calories, it contains 9 g of fat and 3 g of saturated fat or less);
- A maximum of 200 mg of sodium per 100 calories (600 mg of sodium or less for a meal of 300 calories).

If the meal has less than 125 ml of vegetables: add a large salad, a bag of raw vegetables, soup, or vegetable juice. If it does not contain any cheese take your meal with a glass of milk, lean yogurt or a slice of skim milk cheese.

If this is not sufficient to satisfy your appetite: complete it with a slice of buttered whole grain bread or crackers, or a handful of peanuts.

WHO IS IT FOR?

Frozen dinners can be useful for those who live alone, are in a hurry, who are ill, elderly, and do not have the desire, energy, time, motivation or the physical ability necessary to cook.

Substitute dinners

Beverages, powders, and tablets sold as dinner substitutes (*Ensure, Boost, Nutribar*, etc.) share a very lucrative market. This is not surprising, since the latest polls taken by Léger & Léger tell us that more than 1 out of 5 Canadians consume them!

ARE THEY REGULATED?

The composition of meal substitutes is subject to the regulations of Health Canada, particularly with regards to the minimum levels of calories, maximum levels of fat, quality and quantity of protein and the quantity of some twenty vitamins and minerals. As their name implies, meal substitutes are designed to replace a meal, even though paradoxically the federal regulation allows a caloric threshold as low as 225 calories!

WHAT DO THEY CONTAIN?

First and foremost sugar, lots of sugar. Whether it is glucose, fructose, dextrose, syrup, saccharin etc., sugar is almost always the main ingredient.

Also, they contain protein, most often milk and soy. And fat, some good (like canola, sunflower, corn, soy, safflower oils), others not so good (like coconut oil, hydrogenated vegetable oils and cocoa butter).

Chocolate and cocoa are often included for flavor in bars, and rice crisps, nuts, raisins (or other dried fruits) or toasted soy are added for texture.

Finally, a sprinkling of vitamins, minerals and various additives (stabilizing, thickening and emulsifying agents, natural and artificial coloring, etc.) are added. What about the miracle ingredient, the one which will make you lose weight? Don't look for it. When you lose weight with these products it is only because you eat fewer calories!

THE COMPETITION

Nutritional supplements: they are designed not to replace but to supplement a meal, which explains why they generally contain less calories (federal regulations require a minimum of 150 calories), protein, vitamins, or minerals than meal substitutes.

Instant breakfasts: the name leads you to believe they can replace a meal (breakfast), but the regulations as to their contents are far less demanding than those for meal substitutes.

Energy bars: to legally use this name, the federal regulations specify that they must supply at least 100 calories. This is very little.

CAN IT REPLACE A DINNER?

Yes and No…

Regarding calories. A serving of a dinner substitute supplies 250 calories on average, which is far less than what a complete dinner would contain (600-700 calories or more). Unless you wish to suffer hunger pangs, you are more likely to compensate for the lack of calories by snacking an hour later.

From the nutritional point of view. The protein, vitamin and mineral content of a substitute meal can be the equivalent of a regular meal. However, several formulas contain 2 g of fiber or less per meal (the equivalent of approx 250 calories), whereas we should consume 25 to 35 g of fiber per day. But above all, none of these imitations can rival real food which contains hundreds of substances which largely remain to be discovered.

And the taste? Even chocolate can become dull when it is used for every meal! With food, one can vary the pleasure forever…

WHO IS IT FOR?

Meal substitutes may be practical for some people, notably for:

- Those who skip a meal or would eat a chocolate bar or other sweets;
- Those that have difficulties eating enough to fill their nutritional needs, because of:
  - lack of appetite due to illness, death of a loved one, medication, or other reasons;
  - their nutritional needs are higher than normal due to cancer, serious infection, surgery, intestinal absorption problems, etc.

Finally

Fast food, frozen dinners and meal substitutes should only be eaten occasionally or as a temporary solution, since they do not furnish the nutritional needs found in a well-balanced meal.

Chapter 7
Outdoor meals

Summer is the season for outdoor meals. It is also the preferred season for bacteria, which never takes any time off, as proven by the ever increasing number of yearly food poisoning cases. In order to have good memories of your picnic and other outdoor feasts, here are some tips to help you choose, preserve and handle food safely.

Food choices

- **For only one meal or a day.** Go to "Food choices" p.38.
- **For more than a day.** Unless you use a cooler which you can replenish with ice, plan for food which will keep at the surrounding outdoor temperature (see "Safe foods" p. 36). For breakfast, pick dry mixes for crêpes and muffins, ready to serve cereals, bread for toast, liquid eggs in Tetra Pak boxes rather than fresh eggs, bacon or ham. For snacks, some choices are bread, peanut butter, fresh or dried fruits, cereal bars and nuts mix. Powdered milk, juices, soup and milk in Tetra Pak boxes are practical for drinking or cooking.

Take good care

It is important to handle food with care at all times. It is particularly important to do so in hot weather or when the meal will be consumed several hours after being cooked. The tips (given on page 38) and these added precautions will help you.

At preparation time

If you prepare for a picnic or for one day: prepare and refrigerate all you can the night before. Cooling the food ahead (even non-perishables like bread, muffins or fruits) will allow it to stay cool longer in the cooler or the insulated bag.

If you go for more than a day (hiking or camping): freeze everything that can be frozen, perishables or not (meats, deli, cooked meals, sandwiches, bread, muffins, milk, juices etc). It will keep longer and will keep the cooler cold.

When packing
Plan for a cooler with ice or an insulated bag with ice packs.

Pack raw meats in sealed plastic containers. This will prevent their juice from possibly contaminating other foods, especially those not requiring cooking.

Place foods most sensitive to contamination at the bottom of the cooler (see "The risky foods" p. 37). As heat rises and cold descends, they will keep cool longer. Cover these foods with ice packs. Then place less perishable foods, like fruits, raw vegetables, juice boxes, bread or mustard on top. Remember to pack on the bottom the heaviest items and those to be eaten at the end of the meal or day, like dessert and afternoon snack.

Tie containers together. Use string or a scarf (which can be used later as a tablecloth). This will keep the containers from spilling or moving around in the cooler.

Add the freezer packs or ice. A conventional cooler does not make food colder; it only keeps it cold. It is therefore important to place chilled food as well as ice and freezer packs in the cooler. Food will stay cold from 4 to 6 hours. Using only ice keeps food cold from 2 to 4 hours but has the advantage of requiring less space.

On site
Upon arrival at your destination, take the cooler out of the car and place it in the shade. Do not leave it on the back seat of the car or in the trunk, both of which in hot weather can become incubators for bacteria!

Keep the lid closed and avoid opening it needlessly. If space allows, take two coolers, one for perishable foods and the other (usually opened more often) for cold beverages. As to non-perishable items (sun screen, emergency kit, towel, garbage bag), keep them separate.

Cover the cooler with a light colored blanket. It will act as thermal insulation.

Eat in the shade and slip the ice packs under the food containers. The food will remain cold longer.

As soon as the meal is finished, return leftovers to the cooler. Remember that perishable foods should not stay any longer than two hours at room temperature and no more than one hour on a very hot day (32°C or 90°F or more).

Question of weight and space!

We easily consume 1 kilo of food per person daily. This means a lot of food (and equipment) could be used, depending on the number of people and the duration of the hiking or camping trip.

For family meals: limit the choice to a few dishes that will please many rather than several smaller dishes that will take more space. For the same reason it is best to pick family size food containers (juice, milk, yogurt, etc.) rather than individual servings.

For camping or long hikes: plan to pack dehydrated or lyophilized (freeze-dried) foods, and foods requiring little equipment. Avoid preserves. Figure out the exact quantity of food needed. Use plastic bags and dishes, and limit cooking equipment.

The essentials

Pack the following practical items for your trip. They can be kept in a wicker basket or travel bag, separated from perishable food.

- Table cloth (some have a waterproof vinyl coating which is useful if you wish to eat on the grass), clips to keep the table cloth on the table, napkins, plastic utensils and glasses, and for special occasions, plastic wine glasses.
- Hand towels, damp wipes or disposable damp paper towels in a plastic bag.

- A garbage bag to bring back the garbage and some clean plastic bags to bring home the leftover food.
- No toothbrush? Bring sugar-free chewing gum to clean your teeth after your meal.
- And to make the picnic even more pleasant: mosquito netting for the food (to keep insects from annoying us but also from contaminating the food), mosquito repellent, sunscreen, first aid kit, and a camera!

Nothing to bring back!

It is always pleasant to come home fully fed… and empty handed. Here are some tips to return home with no baggage:

- **Non-perishable foods are preferable.** See 'Sure foods' p. 36. Since they can be kept at room temperature for some time, they eliminate the need for freezer packs and thermos bottles.
- **Plan the exact quantities of food.** This is the best way to avoid leftovers and waste.
- **Plan to use disposable packaging.** Use brown paper, waxed paper, plastic film, or sandwich bags rather than thermos

bottles and ice packs. Also, use beverages sold in waxed boxes or in Tetra Pack boxes. Pre-packaged foods are very practical. If utensils are needed (the ideal being to plan for food which can be eaten with one's fingers), use cheap plastic ones.
- **Be careful with very fragile food** (hard cooked eggs, soft fruits, sandwiches, etc.). They are particularly sensitive to impact when not in a rigid container.
- **Make sure there is a place to get rid of your garbage.** If not, have a garbage bag ready to bring it home.

Chapter 8
For happy eating...

With a bit of imagination, a zest of inspiration and a sprinkling of tried and true tips and strategies shown below, you can ensure that your "nice healthy lunch" will end up in your kid's stomach rather than in the garbage! The same could be said for some "adult" lunches...

Label the equipment well. For the precious loot to be found in the right place at the right time, write the name of your child on the lunch box with a waterproof marker or personalized sticker. Do not forget to do the same with the thermos bottle, plastic containers, utensils, cloth napkins, as well as all other accessories, if you want them to find their way home.

Spruce up the equipment. You can apply fun stickers (cartoon characters, stars, little hearts, etc...) to the lunch box, plastic containers and thermos bottles. A serviette, a glass, a straw or a fun napkin will do wonders to stimulate small appetites!

Emphasize (or create) special occasions. Include a small cake for a birthday, a heart shaped cookie for Valentine's Day or pumpkin soup on Halloween. Slip in a drawing, a sticker, a figurine or a Chinese fortune cookie in which you could insert a message. Also you could include in the lunch box a napkin with "happy birthday" on it or "good luck with your test" or simply "see you tonight". There is nothing better than a big grin to facilitate one's digestion!

Do not take any risks. To experiment with new culinary creations for school or day camp meals is risky, especially for a young child! If it is too different or disliked, chances are the child will pass it up and remain hungry. Also it is reassuring for a child to find (in his/her lunch box) familiar food. Of course if sonny only likes ham sandwiches there is nothing wrong with encouraging him to try the ham on a Kaiser, ciabatta bun, or tortilla...

Update the look. Cut the sandwiches and cheese slices or cold meats with a cookie cutter. Carve the raw vegetables with utensils for vegetable decorations. Alternate cheese cubes with fruit chunks on sticks like kebabs. Or superimpose some cheese slices of different colors and cut them in squares, triangles or small sticks. Combine white and whole grain bread for the sandwiches. Roll ham and other cold meat slices and insert in the center a small slice of bell pepper or cheese, small pickle or cooked asparagus. Make a rolled sandwich by using wrap bread, pita or tortilla cut in slices. There are so many ways to give a new look to the traditional.

Vary the textures. When you plan for soft foods — soup, omelet, white sauce, shepherd's pie, macaroni, peanut butter on toast, yogurt, pudding etc. — balance the texture by adding a little crunch. Include in the menu: salad, raw vegetables, whole wheat crackers, stick bread, nuts, granola bar, fresh fruit or fruit sections. Incorporate celery, pickles, or chopped onions with the trimmings for soft sandwiches (ground meat, eggs, cream cheese). Add sprouts, lettuce, or cucumber slices in the sandwiches. As to store bought juice, yogurt and puddings, why not freeze them and enjoy them with a spoon?

Try a breakfast. A guaranteed surprise! A container of Muesli or granola accompanied by a box of milk or yogurt, a muffin, a slice of bread with peanut butter or cheese, toasted waffle or a crepe with freshly cut fruit, an English muffin with egg, ham and cheese (prepared in advance, reheat it at lunch time), a hard cooked egg, sections of orange… are classic breakfasts which can be enjoyed at any time of day.

Offer realistic servings. Does your child return home with packed lunch intact? He may be discouraged by the generous servings involved. Try instead a variety of smaller portions wrapped separately. His pleasure will be immeasurable!

Make life easy. Peel and split oranges in quarters. Cut vegetables and fruits into bite-size pieces (except those which darken, like apples and pears). Cut the sandwiches to manageable size, butter the bread, choose mini vegetables (cherry tomatoes, mini carrots), remove the food from a wrapping too difficult for a child to open… in short, make the task easy for famished little ones.

About the
recipes

The ingredients

The following is the standard we have used for the ingredients to calculate the nutritional values.

Milk and yogurt: milk 1% and yogurt 1%

Eggs: large eggs
Oil: olive oil, unless otherwise indicated
Flour: all purpose flour (white flour)
Stock: store bought powder stock, diluted, unless otherwise indicated

Fresh and dried herbs

In most recipes, one can replace fresh herbs with dried herbs or vice versa by using 2 or 3 times less dried herbs than fresh herbs.

Roasted nuts

Roasting nuts before using them enhances their flavor. When a recipe calls for 'roasted' nuts, roast the quantity indicated in a preheated oven at 180 °C (350 °F) for 10 minutes, or until their aroma comes through or they are lightly colored.

Nutritional values

The nutritional values of most of the recipes in this book are indicated by the following definitions.

Excellent source of...:   the indicated serving supplies 25% (50% for vitamin C) or more of the recommended daily requirement for the mentioned vitamin or mineral, or 6 grams or more of fiber.

Good source of...:   the indicated serving supplies 15% – 24% (30% – 49% for vitamin C) of the recommended daily requirement for the mentioned vitamin and mineral, or 4 – 5.9 grams or more of fiber.

Source of...:   the indicated serving supplies 5% – 14% of the recommended daily requirement for the mentioned vitamin or mineral, or 2 – 3.9 grams of fiber.

Low in fat: the indicated serving supplies 3 grams of fat or less.

Additional information

In most of the recipes there is supplemental information supplied.

Main course   A serving supplies a minimum of 15 g of protein and constitutes the main course.

Quick   The recipe can be made in 15 minutes or less, cooking time included.

Vegetarian   The recipe includes a meat alternative (legumes, tofu, veggie-burger, vegetarian deli, eggs, nuts or grains), but no meat, poultry or fish.

Hot/cold   The meal may be eaten hot or cold.

Can be frozen   Can be made ahead of time and frozen. For more information on the length of recommended freezing time consult the table "Food which can be frozen", p. 23.

Soups

A great way to start a meal! Soups bring warmth and comfort along with a good deal of vitamins, minerals, fluids and often fiber. They also may be a light meal when protein is added. To cut down on sodium, search out a ready-made stock which is salt reduced or salt free or better yet, make your own stock. The amount of sodium in these recipes is calculated using a ready-made stock which is what most people use although it is higher in salt.

Quick Tex-Mex Consommé

Accompanied by a quesadilla, this consommé will transport you to the sunny countryside of Caramba!

2	tortillas 15 cm (6") cut into 1 cm (1/2") strips	2
5 ml	chili powder	1 tsp
2 ml	cumin	1/2 tsp
2 ml	oregano	1/2 tsp
500 ml	chicken stock	2 cups
1	can (284 ml/10 oz) vegetable stock 1 can water	1 plus
1	garlic clove, chopped	1
	dash of Tabasco	
1	can (199 ml/7 oz) whole kernel corn, drained	1
	pepper	
45 ml	chopped coriander or parsley or 15 ml (1 Tbsp) dried parsley	3 Tbsp
	lime quarters (optional)	

Place the tortilla slices on a baking sheet and cook at 200°C (400°F) for 5 minutes or until lightly toasted. Set aside.

In a small skillet heat the chili powder, cumin, and oregano until they smell fragrant. Remove from heat and set aside.

In a large saucepan, mix the stock and water. Add the garlic, reserved spices, Tabasco and the corn. Simmer 5 minutes. Pepper to taste and garnish with coriander.

Variation
For a thicker soup add 1/2 can 540 ml (19 oz) black beans, rinsed and drained.

Tip
Add fresh herbs at the end of the cooking time since they lose much of their nutritional value when heated.

Interesting facts
Coriander has a licorice-like flavor that you either love or hate! It is used especially in Greek, Indian and South American food.

Per serving
Calories 96
Sugars 19 g
Protein 3.4 g
Dietary Fiber 2.1 g
Fat 1.8 g
Sodium 1.301 mg

Source of vitamin A, folic acid, vitamin C, magnesium, iron, and fiber
Low in fat

Clam and Fennel Cream Soup

Main course

What could be more welcoming than a steaming hot soup on a cold winter's day!

| PREPARATION: 10 MIN | COOKING TIME: 20 MIN | 8 SERVINGS 250 ML (1 CUP) |

Variation
Replace the clams with 250 g (1/2 lb) of mussels or chunks of cooked salmon.

Interesting fact
About 60% of the water content is evaporated in evaporated milk. It is slightly colored when compared to fresh milk, with a light caramelized flavor.

Nutritional Information
Evaporated skim milk gives a rich creamy flavor to soups without the calories of cream.

Per serving
Calories 195
Sugars 28 g
Protein 16 g
Dietary Fiber 1.7 g
Fat 2.8 g
Sodium 577 mg

Excellent source of vitamin A, vitamin B12, vitamin C and iron.
Good source of calcium, folic acid, magnesium.
Low in fat

In a saucepan heat oil on medium. Add the onion, fennel, carrots and potatoes and cook, stirring frequently, for 10 minutes or just until the onions are translucent.

Add the stock and the salt, cover and simmer 10 minutes or until the vegetables are tender.

Purée in a food processor. Return purée to saucepan and add the evaporated milk, clams, milk and fennel seeds. Reheat but don't bring to the boil.

Sprinkle with cayenne and garnish with chopped parsley and diced red pepper.

10 ml	oil	2 tsp
1	onion, finely chopped	1
375 ml	(1 small bulb) diced fennel	1 1/2 cups
1	large carrot, diced	1
2	large potatoes, peeled and diced	2
250 ml	chicken or vegetable stock	1 cup
2 ml	salt	1/2 tsp
1	can (385 ml/14 oz) evaporated skim milk	1
2	cans (142 g/5 oz) small clams, drained	2
250 ml	milk	1 cup
1 ml	fennel seeds	1/4 tsp
1	pinch of cayenne	1
45 ml	chopped parsley or 15 ml (1 Tbsp) dried parsley	3 Tbsp
50 ml	red pepper, diced	1/4 cup

Minestrone

This hearty and robust Italian inspired soup, thick and richly colored, is delicious served with pesto and grated parmesan cheese.

PREPARATION: 10 MIN   **COOKING TIME: 20 MIN**   **8 SERVINGS 375 ML (1 1/2 CUPS)**

15 ml	oil	1 Tbsp
1	onion, finely chopped	1
1	clove garlic, finely chopped	1
1	carrot, diced	1
500 ml	chicken or vegetable stock	2 cups
1	can (796 ml/28 oz) diced tomatoes	1
1	can (540 ml/19 oz) chick peas, drained and rinsed	1
1	zucchini, diced	1
125 ml	dried spaghetti, broken up	1/2 cup
15 ml	basil, chopped, or 5 ml (1 tsp) dried basil	1 Tbsp
45 ml	parsley, chopped or 15 ml (1 Tbsp) dried parsley	3 Tbsp
	grated parmesan cheese	

In a saucepan, heat oil on medium. Add the onion, garlic and carrot. Cook for 5 minutes, stirring frequently.

Add the stock and tomatoes and bring to the boil.

Meanwhile, purée 250 ml (1 cup) of the chick peas with 125 ml (1/2 cup) water. Add to soup.

Lower the heat and add the remaining chick peas, the diced zucchini and spaghetti. Simmer for 10 minutes or until the spaghetti is cooked.

Stir in the basil and parsley.

Serve with parmesan cheese.

Tip

For a thinner soup, add tomato juice, stock or water.

By puréeing a portion of the chick peas, it is more appetizing to the finicky eater. Isabelle has proven this with her children who adore this soup.

In most recipes you can replace dried legumes with canned legumes. As they are already cooked, we add them near the end of the cooking time. 250 ml (1 cup) of dry legumes equals 500 to 750 ml (2 to 3 cups) of cooked legumes or a can of 540 ml (19 oz).

Per serving

Calories 165
Sugars 27 g
Protein 7 g
Dietary fiber 3.8 g
Fat 3.6 g
Sodium 565 mg

Excellent source of vitamin A and folic acid
Good source of magnesium and iron
Source of vitamin C, calcium and fiber

Broccoli and Apple Soup

Apple gives a surprising flavor to this soup.

Tip
Peel the stalks of broccoli to remove the tough outer fiber and use peeled stalks in this and other recipes.

Interesting fact
No coloring, salt, preservatives, or other additives are used in frozen vegetables.

Nutritional information
Vegetables to be frozen are gathered at maturity at the height of their flavor and nutritional peak. They are blanched and frozen within three hours of picking. They can be as nutritional as fresh vegetables.

Per serving
Calories 135
Sugars 15 g
Protein 7.3 g
Dietary Fiber 3 g
Fat 5.8 g
Sodium 300 mg

Excellent source of vitamin C
Good source of vitamin A, vitamin B12, folic acid and calcium
Source of magnesium, iron and fiber

In a saucepan heat the oil on medium. Add the leeks and cook, stirring frequently, for 5 minutes or until the leeks are a light golden color.

Add the garlic and cook 1 minute. Incorporate the milk, stock, broccoli, potato and apple and simmer without boiling for 15 minutes or until the vegetables are tender.

Purée in a food processor.

Return purée to saucepan. Salt and pepper to taste.

Reheat gently. Serve, and to each soup bowl add some cream and grated cheddar cheese.

10 ml	oil	2 tsp
2	leeks, whites only, chopped	2
2	cloves garlic, chopped	2
500 ml	milk	2 cups
250 ml	chicken or vegetable stock	1 cup
750 ml	fresh or frozen broccoli in pieces	3 cups
1	potato, peeled and diced	1
1	apple, peeled and diced	1
	salt and pepper	
50 ml	18% cream	1/4 cup
125 ml	extra-old cheddar cheese, grated	1/2 cup

Emerald Soup

Spinach gives a vibrant color to this nourishing soup.
Add a few croutons to give a crunchy texture.

PREPARATION: 10 MIN	COOKING TIME: 20 MIN	5 SERVINGS 250 ML (1 CUP)

10 ml	oil	2 tsp
1	leek or onion, roughly chopped	1
1	potato, peeled and diced	1
1	bag 300 g (10 oz) fresh washed spinach	1
500 ml	chicken or vegetable stock	2 cups
250 ml	milk	1 cup
30 ml	chives, chopped or 10 ml (2 tsp) dried chives	2 Tbsp
	salt and pepper	
50 ml	18% cream	1/2 cup

In a saucepan, heat the oil on medium.

Add the leek or onion and potato. Cook for 5 minutes, stirring frequently.

Add the spinach and stock. Cover and simmer 15 minutes or until the vegetables are tender.

Purée the vegetables in a food processor.

Return the soup to the saucepan and add the milk and chives. Salt and pepper to taste. Reheat gently without boiling.

Swirl 10 ml (2tsp) cream into each serving.

Tip
Thicken soup with puréed potato instead of a rich roux (a mixture of flour and butter).

To wash sand from leeks, cut them to within 2 cm (3/4") of the base and rinse them under cold water while separating the leaves.

Interesting fact
A general rule is the darker the green, the richer a vegetable is in vitamins, minerals and color pigmentation (containing chlorophyll, lutin and beta-carotene) which is associated with the prevention of diseases such as cancer and heart disease.

Per serving
Calories 107
Sugars 12 g
Protein 5.1 g
Dietary fiber 2.5 g
Fat 5 g
Sodium 710 mg

Excellent source of vitamin A, folic acid and magnesium
Good source of vitamin C and iron
Source of vitamin B12, calcium and fiber

Black Olive, Parmesan and Pine Nut Scones

Beef and
Barley Soup

Here's to soup! There is not a better use for leftover beef.
Serve with a hearty slice of country bread.

PREPARATION: 15 MIN	COOKING TIME: 30 MIN	7 SERVINGS 375 ML (1 1/2 CUPS)

15 ml	oil	1 Tbsp
1	leek or onion, roughly chopped	1
1	potato, not peeled, diced	1
2	carrots, sliced	2
750 ml	beef stock	3 cups
1	can (796 ml/28 oz) diced tomatoes	1
1 ml	chili pepper flakes	1/4 tsp
2	bay leaves	2
300 g	cooked beef, cubed	10 oz
125 ml	hulled barley	1/2 cup
50 ml	dry brown lentils (optional)	1/4 cup
50 ml	parsley, chopped or 15 ml (1 Tbsp) dried parsley	1/4 cup
	pepper	

In a saucepan heat the oil on medium. Add the leek or onion, potato and carrots. Cook for 5 minutes, stirring frequently.

Add the stock, tomatoes, chili flakes, and bay leaves and bring to the boil.

Lower the heat, add the beef, barley and lentils and simmer 20 minutes or until the barley is cooked.

Stir in the parsley and pepper and serve.

Nutritional information

Hulled barley is more nutritious than pearl barley where the bran and germ have been removed.

Per serving

Calories 420
Sugars 76 g
Protein 20 g
Dietary fiber 7.7 g
Fats 5.1 g
Sodium 849 mg

Excellent source of vitamin A, vitamin B12, magnesium, iron and fiber
Good source of vitamin C
Source of calcium

Mexican Meatball Soup

This spicy nourishing soup is delicious accompanied by crisp tortilla triangles.

PREPARATION: 15 MIN **COOKING TIME: 25 MIN** **6 SERVINGS 375 ML (1 1/2 CUPS)**

To do ahead
The meatballs may be prepared ahead and frozen.

Tips
For a less "fiery" chili, remove the white membranes and the seeds of the chili pepper while wearing rubber gloves for protection.

For less fat, degrease the soup by letting it cool in the refrigerator and then remove the layer of fat which will have formed on the surface. If you don't have enough time for the soup to cool, skim off as much grease as possible with a small ladle. Next, take a piece of paper toweling and skim it over the surface of the liquid to remove the remaining grease.

Per serving
Calories 323
Sugars 34 g
Protein 22 g
Dietary fiber 3.8 g
Fats 11 g
Sodium 1017 mg

Excellent source of vitamin A and vitamin B12
Good source of folic acid, vitamin C, magnesium and iron
Source of calcium and fiber

In a bowl mix the beef, egg, chili, cumin, chili pepper flakes, chili sauce and wheat germ. Roll into approximately 30 meatballs and refrigerate.

In a skillet, heat the oil on medium. Add the onion, garlic, carrots and chili powder. Cook 5 minutes or just until the onions are translucent.

Add the stock, tomatoes and bay leaf, bring to the boil, add the meatballs and the rice and simmer uncovered for 20 minutes.

Add the kernel corn and reheat gently. Salt and pepper to taste.

500 g	lean ground beef	1 lb
1	egg	1
10 mg	chili powder	2 tsp
5 ml	cumin	1 tsp
1 ml	chili pepper flakes	1/4 tsp
45 ml	chili sauce	3 Tbsp
30 ml	wheat germ or bread crumbs	2 Tbsp
10 ml	oil	2 tsp
1	large onion, chopped	1
2	cloves garlic, finely chopped	2
2	carrots, finely sliced	2
1	jalapeno pepper, seeded and finely chopped (optional)	1
750 ml	beef stock	3 cups
1	can (796 ml/28 oz) diced tomatoes	1
1	bay leaf	1
125 ml	rice, uncooked	1/2 cup
1	can (199 ml/7 oz) whole kernel corn, drained	1
	pepper	

Orange Lentil Soup

This nourishing, delicious orange-flavored soup can also be prepared with 250 ml (1 cup) dried lentils. The cooking time will be almost the same.

PREPARATION: 10 MIN		COOKING TIME: 25 MIN	7 SERVINGS 375 ML (1 1/2 CUPS)

15 ml	oil	1 Tbsp
1	onion, chopped	1
1	leek, white part only, chopped	1
2	celery stalks, diced	2
2	carrots, diced	2
2	garlic cloves, chopped	2
1	can (540 ml/19 oz) tomatoes, diced	1
1	can (540 ml/19 oz) lentils, rinsed and drained	1
1	orange zest strip 8 cm (3") long	1
2 ml	cumin	1/2 tsp
1 L	chicken or vegetable stock	4 cups
1	bay leaf	1
5 ml	oregano	1 tsp
125 ml	parsley, chopped or 45 ml (3 Tbsp) dried parsley	1/2 cup
	pepper	

In a saucepan, heat oil on medium.

Add the onion, leek, celery and carrots, stirring frequently, for 10 minutes or until the vegetables are tender.

Add the garlic and cook 1 minute longer. Stir in the tomatoes, lentils, orange zest, cumin, chicken or vegetable stock, bay leaf and oregano. Simmer, partly covered, for 15 minutes longer.

Remove the zest and the bay leaf. Stir in the parsley, pepper to taste and serve

Tip
Fruits and vegetables are often coated with wax in order to reduce moisture loss. Even though this wax is edible, it is preferable to brush or scrub them under running water. Don't forget that the zest of several citrus fruits can be used in cooking.

Interesting facts
Oregano is a wild variety of marjoram. These two herbs are included in the mix called "Herbs de Provence".

Nutritional information
Eating more vegetables reduces our need to eat as much meat. They are packed with protein, folic acid, iron, magnesium, potassium and fiber. The fat content is negligible and they are cholesterol free.

Per serving
Calories 158
Sugars 26 g
Protein 8.4 g
Dietary fiber 5.4 g
Fats 3.3 g
Sodium 881 mg

Excellent source of vitamin A, folic acid and iron
Good source of vitamin C, magnesium and fiber
Source of calcium

Chicken Noodle Soup

What could be more comforting and fulfilling than a good chicken noodle soup?

PREPARATION: 10 MIN   **COOKING TIME: 25 MIN**   **6 SERVINGS 375 ML (1 1/2 CUPS)**

Variation

For a "chicken and rice" version, replace the noodles with 125 ml (1/2 cup) uncooked rice.

Interesting fact

A good hot chicken noodle soup is a remedy for some cold symptoms. The steam of the broth or certain aromatic ingredients seem to clear the nasal passages. There is nothing to lose by giving it a try!

Per serving

Calories 189
Sugars 15 g
Protein 22 g
Dietary fiber 2.2 g
Fats 4.1 g
Sodium 1260 mg

Excellent source of vitamin A
Good source of folic acid and magnesium
Source of vitamin B12, vitamin C, iron and fiber

In a saucepan heat the oil on medium. Add the onion, carrot, celery and cabbage.

Cook, stirring frequently, for 10 minutes or until the onion is translucent.

Add the stock and bring to the boil. Lower heat, add the chicken and the noodles and simmer for 10 minutes or until the noodles are cooked.

Pepper to taste and stir in the parsley before serving.

10 ml	oil	2 tsp
1	medium onion, diced	1
1	large carrot, diced	1
2	celery stalks, diced	2
250 ml	green cabbage, shredded	1 cup
1.5 L	chicken stock	6 cups
500 ml	cooked chicken, cut into bite size pieces	2 cups
125 ml	small noodles, uncooked	1/2 cup
	Pepper	
30 ml	parsley, chopped or 10 ml (2 tsp) dried parsley	2 Tbsp

Vietnamese Chicken Soup (Pho Ga)

The small amount of sesame oil enhances the taste of this soup enormously without adding much fat.

PREPARATION: 15 MIN	COOKING TIME: 15 MIN	5 SERVINGS 375 ML (1 1/2 CUPS)

1 L	chicken stock	4 cups
500 ml	water	2 cups
2	ginger pieces, 2 cm (3/4") peeled	2
1 ml	chili pepper flakes	1/4 tsp
30 ml	light soy sauce	2 Tbsp
15 ml	oyster sauce (optional)	1 Tbsp
5 ml	toasted sesame oil	1 tsp
375 ml	cooked chicken, finely sliced	1 1/2 cups
6	miniature corn cobs, cut in 2, lengthwise	6
1	carrot, grated	1
500 ml	green or Chinese cabbage, finely sliced	2 cups
1	pkg (85 g/3 oz) instant oriental noodles (dry ramen noodles) without the seasoning pouch	1
45 ml	lemon juice	3 Tbsp
50 ml	green onions, chopped	1/4 cup
6	mint leaves, chopped or 5 ml (1 tsp) dried mint	6
	pepper	

In a saucepan mix the chicken stock, water, ginger, chili pepper flakes, soy sauce, oyster sauce, sesame oil, and chicken, and bring to the boil.

Lower the heat, add the vegetables and simmer 3 minutes. Add the noodles and the lemon juice and stir to separate the noodles. Stir in the green onions and the mint leaves. Pepper to taste and serve.

Variation

Replace the chicken with the same quantity of cooked shrimp or with 250 g (1/2 lb) of extra-firm tofu cut into cubes. Replace the *ramen* noodles with rice vermicelli.

Tip

For less salt, use homemade chicken stock and salt-reduced soy sauce, or dilute the commercial stock more than is suggested in the directions.

Interesting fact

In Vietnam, a soup made with noodles is called Pho while a soup made with rice is called Chai.

Per serving

Calories 200
Sugars 23 g
Protein 21 g
Dietary fiber 1.5 g
Fats 3.1 g
Salt 1441 mg

Excellent source of vitamin A
Good source of vitamin C
Source of vitamin B12, folic acid, magnesium and iron

Vietnamese Chicken Soup (Pho Ga)

Tortellini and Spinach Soup

Can be frozen

You could also prepare this soup using ravioli or gnocchi.
Serve with black olive and pine nut scones (page 130).

PREPARATION: 5 MIN	COOKING TIME: 25 MIN	8 SERVINGS 250 ML (1 CUP)

10 ml	oil	2 tsp
1	large onion, chopped	1
2	garlic cloves, chopped	2
1/2	pkg (300 g/10 oz) chopped frozen spinach	1/2 pkg
1	can (796 ml/28 oz) tomatoes, diced	1
1 L	chicken stock	4 cups
500 ml	uncooked frozen cheese tortellini	2 cups
15 ml	pesto	1 Tbsp
	grated parmesan cheese	

In a saucepan, heat the oil on medium.

Add the onion, garlic and spinach. Cover and cook 10 minutes or until the spinach is defrosted.

Remove the lid and continue cooking for 5 minutes or until the onions are soft.

Add the tomatoes and stock and bring to the boil.

Add the tortellini and cook 10 minutes.

Stir in the pesto and serve with parmesan cheese.

Interesting facts
In Italian, *pesto* means "pulverize" because traditionally, pesto is made by pulverizing the ingredients with a pestle and mortar. A classic pesto is made with basil, but now commercial pesto can be found made with coriander or sun-dried tomatoes.

Nutritional information
Frozen spinach maintains most of the same nutritional quality as fresh spinach: folic acid, iron, calcium, carotene, vitamin C and other nutrients. And best yet, it is already washed!

Per serving
Calories 125
Sugars 17 g
Protein 5.1 g
Dietary fiber 1.9 g
Fats 4.7 g
Sodium 1027 mg

Good source of vitamin A and folic acid
Source of magnesium, calcium and iron

Dressings, Dips and Sauces

The purpose of these nectars is to enhance the taste, appearance and the nutritional value of the dishes that they accompany. Prepare a week's worth in advance and store in the refrigerator in an air-tight container.

Hummus

Traditional hummus is made with chick peas, tahini or sesame butter, garlic, lemon juice and olive oil. Here is a simplified version popular in the Middle East.

PREPARATION: 10 MIN		500 ML (2 CUPS)	
1	can (540 ml/19 oz) chick peas rinsed and drained	1	
45 ml	lemon juice	3 Tbsp	
5 ml	sesame oil	1 tsp	
2 ml	cumin	1/2 tsp	
1 ml	ground coriander	1/4 tsp	
125 ml	water (or more)	1/2 cup	
15 ml	sesame seeds	1 Tbsp	
	salt and pepper		

In a food processor, purée the chick peas, lemon juice, sesame oil, cumin and coriander. Add the water and blend until you obtain the desired texture.

Transfer to a bowl and stir in the sesame seeds. Salt and pepper to taste.

Variation
Add a garlic clove to the processor with the chick peas.

Interesting fact
In certain Middle-East countries, ground coriander is used as a table spice, as we would use salt.

Dried herbs and ground spices keep their flavor and value for about a year. Store them in an air-tight container in a dark place to keep them fresh and dry. Avoid refrigerating them and do not store them in cupboards above the stove.

Per serving of 30 ml
Calories 40
Sugars 6.1 g
Protein 2.0 g
Dietary fiber 0.8 g
Fats 1.1 g
Sodium 2 mg

Good source of folic acid
Source of iron
Low in fat

Avocado
Mayonnaise

Ultra quick to prepare, this mayonnaise can be spread on sandwiches such as grilled chicken or can be used as a vegetable dip.

Tips

Most avocados are not ripe when purchased. When you are planning to use avocados you must buy them ahead of time when they are green and hard. Let them ripen until they are slightly soft to the touch.

Sprinkle the pulp of the avocado with lemon juice or vinegar to avoid darkening of the flesh when exposed to the air. When the mayonnaise is mixed with the avocado pulp there will be some darkening of the surface but the flavor will not be affected. Stir the mixture before serving.

Nutritional information

Although there is fat in avocados, it is the good unsaturated fat.

Per serving of 30 ml

Calories 56
Sugars 4.8 g
Protein 0.5 g
Dietary fiber 0.6 g
Fats 5.3 g
Sodium 38 mg

Source of folic acid

Using a food processor, purée the avocado until it is smooth.

Pour into a bowl and stir in the mayonnaise and lemon juice. Salt and pepper to taste.

1	medium size avocado	1
45 ml	light mayonnaise	3 Tbsp
15 ml	lemon or lime juice	1 Tbsp
	salt and pepper	

Lemon Mayonnaise

Lemons rule! Try this mayonnaise in egg, chicken or tuna sandwiches,
in pasta or potato salads, and even as a vegetable dip or with sesame pita crisps.

PREPARATION: 5 MIN		200 ML (3/4 CUP)

125 ml	plain yogurt	1/2 cup
45 ml	light mayonnaise	3 Tbsp
10 ml	lemon juice	2 tsp
30 ml	parsley, chopped	2 Tbsp
30 ml	chives, chopped	2 Tbsp
1 ml	lemon zest	1/4 tsp
	salt and pepper	

Sesame pita crisps

4	pitas	4
	cooking oil spray	
	sesame seeds	

In a bowl mix the yogurt, mayonnaise, lemon juice, parsley, chives and lemon zest. Salt and pepper to taste.

For the sesame pita crisps, separate the two pita layers. Cut each layer into quarters. Spray each triangle with oil and sprinkle with sesame seeds. Bake in an oven preheated to 200°C (400°F) for 5 minutes or until the triangles are crisp and golden.

Variation
Add two finely chopped garlic cloves to obtain a fast lemon aïoli, a mayonnaise of Provence which is delicious served with chicken.

Tips
Add curry, chili powder or paprika to the mayonnaise and spread it over skinless chicken breasts and roast in the oven. It is divine!
Rather than searching around in your lunch bag or box for the small container of mayonnaise, put it in the center of the salad or sandwich container, or tape it to the lid.

Per serving of 30 ml
Calories 34
Sugars 2.2 g
Protein 1.1 g
Dietary fiber 0.1 g
Fats 2.4 g
Sodium 59 mg

Source of vitamin B12
Low in fat

Sweet and Sour Sauce

The secret is in the sauce! Very versatile, this sauce is delicious with pork chops, chicken breasts, ham steaks or chicken croquettes. It can also serve as a marinade for meat or poultry.

PREPARATION: 5 MIN   **COOKING TIME: 5 MIN**   **300 ML (1 1/4 CUPS)**

Per serving of 30 ml
Calories 35
Sugars 8.4 g
Protein 0.4 g
Dietary fiber 0.1 g
Fats 0.0 g
Sodium 62 mg

Source of folic acid and vitamin C
No fat content

In a bowl, mix the corn starch with the orange juice.

Add the soy sauce, plum sauce, sugar and garlic. Spice up the flavor by adding a dash or so of Tabasco sauce.

Pour the sauce into a nonstick skillet and cook on medium heat, while stirring constantly, until it comes to the boil.

Lower the heat and simmer 5 minutes or until the sauce thickens.

30 ml	corn starch	2 Tbsp
250 ml	orange juice or mango and orange	1 cup
15 ml	soy sauce	1 Tbsp
50 ml	Chinese plum sauce	1/4 cup
15 ml	honey or sugar	1 Tbsp
2	garlic cloves, finely chopped	2
	dash of Tabasco sauce	

Remoulade Sauce

This remoulade can be served with cooked fish, used as a dressing or as a spread with sandwiches.

PREPARATION: 5 MIN		150 ML (2/3 CUP)
45 ml	light mayonnaise	3 Tbsp
50 ml	tomatoes, chopped	1/4 cup
1	green onion, chopped	1
30 ml	plain yogurt	2 Tbsp
2 ml	hot mustard	1/2 tsp
10 ml	capers, chopped	2 tsp
2 ml	Worcestershire sauce	1/2 tsp
	pepper	

In a small bowl, mix all the ingredients. Pepper to taste.

Interesting facts

Worcestershire sauce, an English condiment, is made of malt vinegar, molasses, shallots, garlic, tamarind paste, cloves, anchovy oil and meat extract.

Capers are the flower buds of the caper bush, a perennial native to the Mediterranean region. The smaller the caper, the more tender, the more delicately flavored, the more aromatic, and the more expensive they are.

Per serving of 30 ml

Calories 34
Sugars 1.7 g
Protein 0.5 g
Dietary fiber 0.1 g
Fats 2.9 g
Sodium 109 mg

Low in fat

Mushroom Dip

"More vegetables!" the children cry. For a change from the traditional white mushrooms (champignons de Paris) replace a part of them with wild mushrooms.

Variation

Incorporate 50 ml (1/4 cup) roasted, chopped walnuts or pecans for a crunchy texture.

Tips

Store mushrooms in a paper bag or perforate the plastic covering to get rid of humidity and to preserve their freshness. Refrigerate them without cleaning.

For an incomparable flavor, grind 2 or 3 dried mushrooms to a powder and add to the dip. Wait at least 30 minutes before eating to allow the flavor to develop.

Per serving of 30 ml

Calories 33
Sugars 1.8 g
Protein 1.3 g
Dietary fiber 0.2 g
Fats 1.8 g
Sodium 51 mg

Low in fat

In a skillet, sauté the onion, mushrooms and thyme in the oil until the vegetable liquids have evaporated.

Transfer this to a bowl and mix in the yogurt, cream cheese, sour cream and mayonnaise until the mixture is homogenous. Salt and pepper to taste.

Cut the tortillas into strips and place them under the grill for approximately 3 minutes or until they are crisp.

Serve the mushroom dip with the tortilla crisps and veggies.

5 ml	oil	1 tsp
50 ml	red onion, chopped	1/4 cup
375 ml	mushrooms, chopped	1 1/2 cups
1 ml	thyme	1/4 tsp
125 ml	plain yogurt	1/2 cup
50 ml	low fat cream cheese, softened	1/4 cup
50 ml	low fat sour cream	1/4 cup
15 ml	light mayonnaise	1 Tbsp
	Salt and pepper	
3	tortillas 25 cm (10") in diameter	3
	a variety of raw veggies	

Peanut Dip

This Asian sauce is one that "peanut butter lovers" will appreciate.

PREPARATION: 5 MIN   **75 ML (1/3 CUP)**

30 ml	creamy peanut butter	2 Tbsp
15 ml	light soy sauce	1 Tbsp
15 ml	light mayonnaise	1 Tbsp
15 ml	brown sugar	1 Tbsp
15 ml	lemon juice	1 Tbsp

In a bowl, mix all the ingredients. If the dip is too thick, add 15 to 30 ml (1-2 Tbsp) water.

Nutritional information

Either regular or natural peanut butter is a good choice for this recipe. Regular peanut butter has hydrogenated oil or "bad fat" added, which inhibits the oil from separating and going to the surface.

Per serving of 30 ml

Calories 122
Sugars 9.6 g
Protein 3.9 g
Dietary fiber 0.8 g
Fat 8.4 g
Sodium 274 mg

Source of magnesium

Avocado Mayonnaise   Mushroom Dip   Peanut Dip   81

Cranberry Dressing

Eat color! It is healthy feel-good food. The red pigment (anthocyanin) of cranberries help inhibit production of cholesterol by the body.

PREPARATION: 10 MIN		200 ML (3/4 CUP)
45 ml	oil	3 Tbsp
10 ml	balsamic vinegar	2 tsp
10 ml	old-style mustard (*à l'ancienne*)	2 tsp
75 ml	orange juice	1/3 cup
30 ml	dried cranberries	2 Tbsp
5 ml	orange zest	1 tsp
	salt and pepper	

In the food processor, add the oil, vinegar, mustard, orange juice, cranberries and orange zest. Pulse the blade just until the cranberries are finely chopped. Salt and pepper to taste.

Interesting facts

Cranberries help prevent and treat urinary infections. Their proanthocyanidines, (a type of tannin), inhibit bacteria from sticking to the urinary tract, multiplying, and causing infection.

In traditional Italian cuisine, salt is sprinkled directly on the lettuce before adding any other ingredient. It is unbelievable how a little salt added this way can add to the flavor of the salad.

Per serving of 30 ml

Calories 68
Sugars 2.0 g
Protein 0.1 g
Dietary fiber 0.2 g
Fats 4.3 g
Sodium 13 mg

Source of vitamin C

Pizzaiolla Dressing

This dressing came by its name because of its pizza ingredients.
It is delicious with pasta salad or a simple green salad.

200 ML (3/4 CUP)

In a bowl mix all ingredients until they are well combined. Salt and pepper to taste.

1	can (156 ml/5.5 oz) tomato juice	1
30 ml	wine vinegar	2 Tbsp
15 ml	oil	1 Tbsp
5 ml	oregano	1 tsp
5 ml	dried basil	1 tsp
2 ml	sugar	1/2 tsp
1	garlic clove, finely chopped	1
	salt and pepper	

Sweet Red Pepper Dressing

This is super with pasta salad topped with tuna and white onion rings!

PREPARATION: 10 MIN		250 ML (1 CUP)
1	jar (198 ml/7 oz) roasted red peppers, rinsed and drained	1
50 ml	plain yogurt	1/4 cup
5 ml	basil, chopped or 1 ml (1/4 tsp) dried basil	1 tsp
15 ml	oil	1 Tbsp
10 ml	lemon juice	2 tsp
1	garlic clove	1
	salt and pepper	

In the food processor, blend ingredients to a smooth purée. Salt and pepper to taste.

Tips

Mix 30 ml (2 Tbsp) of this dressing with a can (170 g/6oz) of tuna and you have a quick sandwich filling.

To test the flavor of a dressing, taste it with one of the salad ingredients such as lettuce or a vegetable to make sure that it is not overpowering.

Interesting facts

Green peppers turn red when they are left to ripen on the plant. Because they are picked early, travel well and have a longer shelf life, they are less expensive than red peppers.

Per serving (30 ml)

Calories 22
Sugars 1.3 g
Protein 0.4 g
Dietary fiber 0.1 g
Fat 1.8 g
Sodium 5 mg

Good source of vitamin C
Low in fat

Sweet Red Pepper Dressing

Thousand Island Dressing

This delicious rose dressing is sensational with a green salad.

PREPARATION: 10 MIN	300 ML (1 1/4 CUPS)

125 ml	plain yogurt	1/2 cup
125 ml	1% sour cream	1/2 cup
50 ml	chili sauce	1/4 cup
15 ml	onion, finely chopped	1 Tbsp
15 ml	carrots, finely grated	1 Tbsp
5 ml	lemon juice	1 tsp
1 ml	pepper	1/4 tsp

Put all ingredients in the bowl of the food processor and purée until homogenized.

Alternatively, all of the ingredients could be beaten together using a wire whisk.

Interesting fact
Commercial dressings cost at least five times as much as the home-made versions.

Nutritional information
Some commercial dressings contain approximately 200 calories, 20 g of fat and 500 mg of sodium per modest portion of 30 ml (2 Tbsp)! Look for those where the label lists 300 mg or less of sodium and 6 g of fat (approximately 8 ml/1/2 Tbsp oil) per serving of 30 ml (2 Tbsp).

Per serving
Calories 33
Sugars 2.9 g
Protein 1.1 g
Dietary fiber 0.0 g
Fats 1.9 g
Sodium 79 mg

Source of vitamin B12
Low in fat

Vegetables, Legumes and Salads

Consuming an abundance of plant foods reduces the principal causes of disease and death including cancer and heart disease. Here are some innovative ways to eat a little more "veggie"!

Duo Colored Potato Gratin Dauphinois

Can be frozen

A great classic updated thanks to adding sweet potatoes.
This is delicious accompanied with tomato meat loaf (see page 156).

PREPARATION: 15 MIN	COOKING TIME: 40 MIN	8 SERVINGS

4	medium potatoes, peeled and finely sliced	4
2	sweet potatoes, peeled and finely sliced	4
1	medium onion, sliced sliver thin	1
75 ml	flour	1/3 cup
7 ml	salt	1 1/2 tsp
1 ml	pepper	1/4 tsp
1 ml	nutmeg	1/4 tsp
1	can (385 ml/14 oz) evaporated skimmed milk	1
125 ml	milk	1/2 cup
200 ml	old cheddar or gruyère cheese, grated	3/4 cup

Preheat the oven to 200°C (400°F).

Place the vegetables in a large bowl. Sprinkle with flour and add the salt, pepper and nutmeg. Mix well in order to coat the vegetables.

Place this preparation in a heat-proof casserole dish 25 cm x 35 cm (9" x 13"). Pour the evaporated milk and milk on the vegetables and top with cheese.

Cover and bake for 40 minutes or until the vegetables are cooked, then remove the cover and place under the broiler for a few minutes until the top is bubbling and golden.

Tips

Get two birds with one stone. The potato gratin and the tomato meat loaf have almost the same cooking time and their flavors make for a great combination. Cook them together.

The flesh of sweet potatoes darkens as soon as they are cut. It is best to keep them in cold water or cook them immediately.

Nutritional information

The sweet potato is one of the vegetables highest in beta-carotene which gives it its rich orange color. It is also a good source of vitamin C.

Per serving

Calories 185
Sugars 28 g
Protein 9.2 g
Dietary fiber 2.1 g
Fats 4.3 g
Sodium 548 mg

Excellent source of vitamin A
Good source of vitamin C and calcium
Source of vitamin B12, folic acid, magnesium, iron and fiber

Duo Colored Potato Gratin Dauphinois

Spiced Chick Pea Ragoût

When served on a nest of basmati rice, this is a nutritious, flavorful and economical meal! This ragoût (stew) can be refrigerated for up to 4 days.

PREPARATION: 10 MIN	COOKING TIME: 25 MIN	4 SERVINGS 250 ML (1 CUP)

10 ml	oil	2 tsp
1	large onion, chopped	1
2	large garlic cloves, finely chopped	2
1	small zucchini, diced	1
10 ml	ginger, peeled and chopped	2 tsp
5 ml	cumin	1 tsp
5 ml	turmeric	1 tsp
10 ml	ground coriander	2 tsp
1 ml	red chili flakes	1/4 tsp
1	sweet potato, peeled and diced	1
1	can (540 ml/19 oz) chick peas, rinsed and drained	1
1	can (213 ml/7 1/2 oz) tomato sauce, plus the same amount of water	1
30 ml	lemon or lime juice	2 Tbsp
	salt and pepper	
	coriander, chopped (optional)	

In a large saucepan, heat the oil and sauté the onion, garlic and zucchini for 5 minutes or until the onions are softened.

Add the ginger, cumin, turmeric, coriander and the chili flakes and sauté approximately 1 minute until fragrant.

Add the diced sweet potatoes, chick peas, and tomato sauce and bring to the boil.

Lower the heat and let simmer 20 minutes or until the sweet potato is cooked. Stir in the lemon. Salt and pepper to taste and sprinkle with chopped coriander.

Variation
For a more or less spicy taste, add or reduce the quantity of ginger and chili flakes.

Tip
The fresh ginger can be replaced by ground ginger but the taste will not be the same. When purchasing ginger look for a firm rhizome, not shriveled and dry.

Nutritional information
Basmati rice is a fine, long-grained rice with a silky texture. Its delicate perfume makes it an ideal and indispensable accompaniment to Indian dishes.

Per serving
Calories 232
Sugars 40 g
Protein 10 g
Dietary fiber 5.9 g
Fats 5.0 g
Sodium 326 mg

Excellent source of vitamin A, folic acid, magnesium and iron
Good source of vitamin C and fiber
Source of calcium

Roasted Lentils

Main dish · Can be frozen · Vegetarian

When made with lentils rather than white navy beans, this recipe is a change from the traditional "baked beans".

PREPARATION: 35 MIN	COOKING TIME: 2 HOURS	5 SERVINGS 250 ML (1 CUP)

Tips

In order to let legumes tenderize during cooking, don't add salt or acid ingredients (tomatoes, wine or lemon juice) until near the end of cooking. Always rinse dry legumes in cold water, removing any that are discolored, cracked or broken, as well as any stones or grit. Lentils do not need soaking before cooking.

To reduce flatulence, add a few sprigs of savory or sage leaves to the cooking water of legumes.

Per serving

Calories 283
Sugars 53 g
Protein 16 g
Dietary fiber 7.3 g
Fats 1.2 g
Sodium 574 mg

Excellent source of folic acid, magnesium, iron and fiber
Source of vitamin C and calcium
Low in fat

Preheat oven to 190°C (375°F).

Put the lentils in a sieve and rinse them under cold water. In a large saucepan combine the water and lentils. Bring to the boil, cover, and simmer for 30 minutes.

Drain the lentils and reserve 250 ml (1 cup) of the cooking liquid. Put the lentils and onion in a 2 L (8 cup) bean pot or casserole.

In another bowl, combine the reserved cooking liquid, chili sauce, molasses, dry mustard and chili flakes. Pour over the lentils, add 500 ml (2 cups) water and mix well. Cover and roast for 1 hour in the preheated oven.

Remove the lid and cook an additional hour. Add water if needed. When the lentils are cooked, add salt and pepper to taste.

500 ml	dried brown lentils	2 cups
1.5 L	water	6 cups
1	large onion, chopped	1
150 ml	chili sauce	2/3 cup
50 ml	molasses	1/4 cup
15 ml	dry mustard	1 Tbsp
1 ml	dried chili flakes	1/4 tsp
2 ml	salt	1/2 tsp
	pepper	

Red Lentil and Bulgur Pilaf

This dry mixture can be kept frozen for several months, and can serve as a quick breakfast or lunch! Add water and 10 minutes later lunch is served!

PREPARATION: 5 MIN   **COOKING TIME: 10 MIN**   **4 SERVINGS 200 ML (3/4 CUP)**

45 ml	sunflower seeds	3 Tbsp
125 ml	dried red lentils	1/2 cup
125 ml	uncooked bulgur	1/2 cup
30 ml	dried apricots, chopped	2 Tbsp
30 ml	raisins	2 Tbsp
10 ml	oil	2 tsp
1	large piece of orange zest	1
1	bay leaf	1
5 ml	cumin	1 tsp
2 ml	ground ginger	1/2 tsp
1 ml	dried chili flakes	1/4 tsp
1	chicken or vegetable bouillon cube	1
550 ml	water	2 1/4 cups

In an air-tight container or zip-lock bag, combine all the ingredients except the water. You can freeze this mix, take it to work as is, or cook it immediately.

To cook

In a medium size saucepan, bring the water to a boil, add the pilaf, stir, cover and cook on low heat until the water has been almost absorbed, about 10 minutes. Remove the orange zest and bay leaf. Serve with pita bread or a naan along with mint carrot salad (see page 102).

Tip

To obtain fine strips of orange or lemon zest, use a zester, a short-handled utensil equipped with one to five small holes. Also, you could use a paring knife to cut large bands of zest. Be careful not to include any white pith when zesting because of its bitter taste.

Nutritional information

Because dried fruits have less moisture than fresh fruit, they are a concentrated source of vitamins, minerals and energy.

The legume and cereal duo in this lentil and bulgur recipe has a protein content equal to that of meat.

Per serving

Calories 206
Sugars 33 g
Protein 9.1 g
Dietary fiber 6.7 g
Fats 5.5 g
Sodium 425 mg

Excellent source of folic acid, magnesium and fiber
Good source of iron

Red Lentil and Bulgur Pilaf

93

Fennel and Orange Salad

Quick

Here is a simple preparation of fennel to bring out its sweet licorice flavor.
This salad will keep up to 3 days refrigerated.

PREPARATION: 10 MIN		4 SERVINGS 250 ML (1 CUP)
1	small fennel bulb, finely sliced	1
2	oranges, peeled, removing skin and pith and cut into small pieces	2
15 ml	chives, chopped or 5 ml (1 tsp) dried chives	1 Tbsp
15 ml	wine or balsamic vinegar	1 Tbsp
15 ml	oil	1 Tbsp
	salt and pepper	

Put the fennel, orange pieces and chives in a small bowl.

Pour on the vinegar, oil and seasoning. Toss thoroughly.

Variation
For a light meal, add canned tuna or salmon.

Tip
To peel an orange or grapefruit ensuring that the pith is removed, cut off each end and with a serrated knife, remove the peel and pith (white part) in one motion by cutting it away in sections from top to bottom, exposing the flesh of the orange.

Nutritional information
Fennel is a long white or pale green bulb topped by green feathery stalks. It has a delicate anise or licorice flavor. When buying, look for a firm sweet smelling bulb free of blemishes and with fresh greenery. It keeps well for up to 1 week refrigerated.

Per serving
Calories 79
Sugars 12 g
Protein 1.3 g
Dietary fiber 1.2 g
Fats 3.7 g
Sodium 28 mg

Excellent source of vitamin C
Good source of folic acid
Source of magnesium

Crunchy Vegetables Seasoned with Balsamic Vinegar

This colorful and flavorful salad is chock-full of vitamins.

PREPARATION: 15 MIN **3 SERVINGS 250 ML (1 CUP)**

Variety
For a Mediterranean flair, add shaved fresh parmesan cheese which is easy to do using a vegetable peeler.

Tip
To avoid pine nuts going rancid, store in the freezer for 2-3 months or refrigerate up to one month.

Nutritional information
Balsamic vinegar is made by harvesting very ripe sweet white grapes, usually the trebbiano grape. As it ferments it is decanted into a succession of different barrels made of various kinds of wood. It is this process which produces its slightly acidic flavor, brown color and somewhat syrupy consistency.

Per serving
Calories 96
Sugars 9.3 g
Protein 3.2 g
Dietary fiber 2.9 g
Fats 6.5 g
Sodium 7 mg

Excellent source of vitamin C
Good source of folic acid
Source of vitamin A, magnesium, iron and fiber

Cook the green beans in salted, boiling water for 3 minutes. Rinse in cold water.

Cut into 2 cm (3/4") pieces and put in a salad bowl. Incorporate the remaining ingredients except for the pine nuts and mix gently with the green beans.

Garnish with pine nuts. Salt and pepper to taste.

250 ml	green beans	1 cup
1/2	sweet red pepper, cut in strips	1/2
1	small yellow zucchini, diced	1
125 ml	mushrooms, thinly sliced	1/2 cup
1	green onion, chopped	1
15 ml	oil	1 Tbsp
15 ml	balsamic vinegar	1 Tbsp
5 ml	basil, chopped or 2 ml (1/2 tsp) dried basil	1 tsp
15 ml	pine nuts, toasted	1 Tbsp
	salt and pepper	

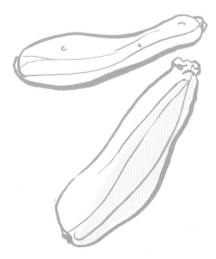

Melon and Cucumber Salad

The slightly peppery flavor of watercress goes well with the sweetness
of the melon in this "green" salad, which will keep well refrigerated for 2 days.

PREPARATION: 15 MIN		4 SERVINGS 300 ML (1 1/4 CUPS)
750 ml	honeydew melon, diced	3 cups
250 ml	cucumber, diced	1 cup
250 ml	watercress leaves	1 cup
15 ml	oil	1 Tbsp
15 ml	mint, chopped or 5 ml (1 tsp) dried mint	1 Tbsp
15 ml	honey	1 Tbsp
15 ml	white wine or cider vinegar	1 Tbsp
	pepper	

Put the melon, cucumber and watercress in a bowl and toss gently.

Combine the sauce ingredients and pour on the salad. Pepper to taste.

Tips

Watercress or cress is sold by the bunch. Preserve in the refrigerator by putting the stalks in water as you would a bouquet. For a wonderful flavor, add the leaves to salads and the stems to soup.

If honey has solidified or crystallized, liquefy it by putting it in the microwave and heating on high for several seconds.

Interesting fact

Cold dishes need to be more highly seasoned than hot dishes since the cold diminishes the intensity of flavors.

Per serving

Calories 105
Sugars 19 g
Protein 1.1 g
Dietary fiber 1.6 g
Fats 3.8 g
Sodium 19 mg

Excellent source of vitamin C
Good source of folic acid
Source of vitamin A and magnesium

"Quills" and Chicken with Fruit and Curry

This exotic gourmet delight will certainly transport you to India even though one of the main ingredients is Italian penne, which means quills.

PREPARATION: 15 MIN	COOKING TIME: 10 MIN	5 SERVINGS 375 ML (1 1/2 CUPS)

Variation

Replace the pasta with 750 ml (3 cups) cooked rice. Replace the creamy dressing with a mixture of 60 ml (4 Tbsp) apple cider vinegar, 45 ml (3 Tbsp) oil, 15 ml (1 Tbsp) curry, and 5 ml (1 tsp) hot mustard.

Nutritional information

Whether they are fresh or dry, apricots contain a high amount of carotenoid (the pigmentation which gives them their yellow-orange color), which acts as a potent antioxidant.

Per Serving

Calories 423
Sugars 51 g
Protein 28 g
Dietary fiber 3.5 g
Fats 12 g
Sodium 254 mg

Excellent source of magnesium
Good source of vitamin B12 and iron
Source of vitamin A, folic acid, vitamin C, calcium and fiber

Cook the pasta in a large pot of boiling salted water until the pasta is *al dente*. Rinse with cold water and set aside.

In a small nonstick pan, dry-fry the almonds approximately 5 minutes until they release their nutty aroma and turn golden. Set aside.

In a large bowl, place the chicken, celery, apricots, green onions, raisins and diced potatoes.

Put the curry in a small bowl and add the mayonnaise, yogurt and mustard. Salt and pepper to taste. Mix well.

Pour the dressing over the salad ingredients and toss gently. Garnish with the toasted almonds.

500 ml	uncooked penne or fusilli	2 cups
30 ml	slivered almonds	2 Tbsp
500 ml	cooked chicken, diced	2 cups
125 ml	celery, diced	1/2 cup
125 ml	dried apricots, thick sliced	1/2 cup
2	green onions, chopped	2
50 ml	raisins	1/4 cup
1	unpeeled red apple, diced	1

Creamy dressing

15 ml	curry	1 Tbsp
125 ml	light mayonnaise	1/2 cup
200 ml	plain yogurt	3/4 cup
5 ml	hot mustard	1 tsp
	salt and pepper	

New Potatoes with Lemon-Chive Vinaigrette

Fresh squeezed lemon is the secret for this potato salad without mayonnaise!

PREPARATION: 15 MIN	COOKING TIME: 10 MIN	6 SERVINGS 375 ML (1 1/2 CUPS)

6	unpeeled new potatoes, scrubbed	6
250 ml	snow peas, cut on the diagonal	1 cup
250 ml	frozen green peas	1 cup
3	green onions, chopped	3
1/2	sweet red pepper, diced	1/2

Vinaigrette

50 ml	extra virgin olive oil	1/4 cup
50 ml	lemon juice	1/4 cup
30 ml	chives, chopped	2 Tbsp
2 ml	sugar	1/2 tsp
	salt and pepper	

Cook the potatoes in salted boiling water for 10 to 15 minutes or until they are tender. Rinse in cold water. Cut potatoes into medium thick slices and let cool in a large bowl.

Meanwhile cook the snow peas in salted boiling water for 3 minutes, then add the frozen green peas and cook 2 minutes more. Rinse in cold water. Add the potatoes.

Pour on the vinaigrette and gently mix in the green onions and red peppers. Salt and pepper to taste.

Variation

This salad can be a main course with the addition of hard cooked eggs, tuna, salmon or canned shrimp.

For a heartier salad, add 30 ml (2 Tbsp) Roquefort cheese and 2 slices of crisp, cooked and crumbled bacon. Drizzle the salad with a tea vinaigrette: 50 ml (1/4 cup) cold black tea, 45 ml (3 Tbsp) lemon juice, 15 ml (1 Tbsp) oil, 15 ml (1 Tbsp) wine vinegar, and salt and pepper to taste.

Tip

Plan ahead to have about 1.25 L (5 cups) leftover potatoes that could be "recycled" by cutting into thick slices for this salad.

Per serving

Calories 283
Sugars 48 g
Protein 6.4 g
Dietary fiber 6.2 g
Fats 7.9 g
Sodium 39 mg

Excellent source of vitamin C, magnesium and fiber
Good source of folic acid and iron
Source of vitamin A

Rice and Black Bean Mexican Salad

Some tomato slices, a lemon quarter and a tortilla would be a marvelous accompaniment to this unusual salad. Add a few drops of Tabasco to the dressing for a spicier flavor! This salad will last 4 days in the refrigerator.

PREPARATION: 15 MIN　　　**6 SERVINGS 300 ML (1 1/4 CUP)**

Variation
Replace the black beans with an equal quantity of red kidney beans or green lentils.

Nutritional information
Beans cause flatulence? Be careful to rinse canned beans well, as well as cooked dried ones. Cook beans until they can easily be crushed by a fork. Avoid desserts or other sweets at the same meal. Be patient: the digestive system adapts to beans with time.

Per serving
Calories 245
Sugars 41 g
Protein 9.7 g
Dietary fiber 6.1 g
Fats 5.7 g
Sodium 186 mg

Excellent source of folic acid, magnesium and fiber
Good source of iron
Source of vitamin A and vitamin C

In a bowl, mix the first 6 ingredients and set aside.

In a small bowl, mix the lemon juice, salt, pepper and cumin. Incorporate the oil in a fine stream, whipping all the while, until the vinaigrette thickens.

Add the parsley and garlic cloves.

Pour on the salad and toss gently.

1	can (540 ml/19 oz) black beans, rinsed and drained	1
1	can (199 ml/7 oz) whole kernel corn, drained	1
500 ml	brown rice, cooked	2 cups
250 ml	frozen green peas, cooked	1 cup
1	large tomato, diced	1
1	small yellow zucchini, diced	1
45 ml	lemon juice	3 Tbsp
2 ml	salt	1/2 tsp
1 ml	pepper	1/4 tsp
5 ml	cumin	1 tsp
30 ml	oil	2 Tbsp
50 ml	parsley, chopped or 15 ml (1 Tbsp) dried parsley	1/4 cup
2	garlic cloves, finely chopped	2

Tofu Greek Salad

A traditional dish to which tofu is added for extra protein.

PREPARATION: 15 MIN   **WAITING TIME: 20 MIN**   **3 SERVINGS 750 ML (3 CUPS)** (OF WHICH 250 ML/1 CUP IS MIXED WITH TOF

1	bunch red leaf lettuce or frisée, torn up or 1 small head of romaine, torn up	1
75 ml	feta cheese, crumbled	1/3 cup
1	small red onion, chopped	1
125 ml	pitted black olives, chopped	1/2 cup
30 ml	lemon juice	2 Tbsp
30 ml	oil	2 Tbsp
5 ml	oregano	1 tsp
250 ml	firm tofu, crumbled	1 cup
	salt and pepper	
2	red tomatoes, diced	2
1	pita (18 cm/7") sliced in strips and grilled	1

Put the lettuce in a salad bowl and set aside.

In a bowl, mix the feta, onion, olives, lemon juice, oil and oregano.

Add the tofu and crush with a fork in order to blend all the ingredients. Salt and pepper to taste.

Cover and refrigerate for 20 minutes, or refrigerate until the next day.

Just before serving, add the diced tomatoes to the tofu mixture and place on the lettuce.

Garnish with grilled pita strips.

Variation

Replace the feta with 125 ml (1/2 cup) of another strong tasting cheese such as shaved fresh parmesan cheese or grated old cheddar cheese.

Use the tofu mixture as a sandwich filling in pitas.

Nutritional information

Since feta cheese is preserved in brine, it keeps for several months refrigerated, when handled with care. Its characteristic flavor is pronounced and slightly sharp.

Per serving

Calories 311
Sugars 25 g
Protein 14 g
Dietary fiber 4.7 g
Fats 19 g
Sodium 415 mg

Excellent source of vitamin A, folic acid, vitamin C, magnesium, calcium and iron
Good source of vitamin B12 and fiber

Tofu Greek Salad

Mint Carrot Salad

This salad has a refreshing quality due to the mint.
It keeps 4 days in the refrigerator.

PREPARATION: 10 MIN		4 SERVINGS 200 ML (3/4 CUP)
45 ml	light mayonnaise	3 Tbsp
45 ml	plain yogurt	3 Tbsp
5 ml	hot mustard	1 tsp
15 ml	fresh mint, chopped or 5 ml (1 tsp) dried mint	1 Tbsp
750 ml	carrots, grated	3 cups
	salt and pepper	

In a bowl mix the mayonnaise, yogurt, mustard and mint. Salt and pepper to taste.

Fold in the grated carrots.

Tip
Good news: you can now purchase bags of grated carrots!

Nutritional information
The deep orange color of carrots, sweet potatoes, pumpkin and cantaloupe is a sign of their rich beta-carotene content, an antioxidant well known to be a cancer and heart disease preventative.

Per serving
Calories 86
Sugars 12 g
Protein 1.7 g
Dietary fiber 2.3 g
Fats 4.1 g
Sodium 139 mg

Excellent source of vitamin A
Source of folic acid, vitamin C, magnesium and fiber

Celery Root Salad with Orange Dressing

This crisp, multi-colored salad served with a tender piece of fish makes a great little meal!
This salad will be even more flavorful the next day. It will keep up to 4 days refrigerated.

PREPARATION: 20 MIN　　　　**5 SERVINGS 200 ML (3/4 CUP)**

Tip
To avoid oxidization or darkening of the celery root, sprinkle with lemon juice or salad dressing as soon as it is cut and grated.

Nutritional information
Celery root is a large round, whitish root resembling a large turnip. It has the flavor of celery (even a little more pronounced) without the fibrous quality.

Per serving
Calories 203
Sugars 19 g
Protein 2.1 g
Dietary fiber 1.8 g
Fats 14 g
Sodium 120 mg

Excellent source of folic acid and vitamin C
Source of magnesium and iron

Pour the juice in the bowl of a food processor along with the vinegar, mustard and orange zest.

Blend until it is homogenous and, while the motor is running, add the oil in a fine stream.

Incorporate the dressing and parsley with the celery root.

Salt and pepper to taste.

Dressing

125 ml	non-diluted frozen orange concentrate	1/2 cup
15 ml	white wine vinegar	1 Tbsp
15 ml	hot mustard	1 Tbsp
2 ml	orange zest	1/2 tsp
75 ml	extra virgin olive oil	1/3 cup
30 ml	parsley, chopped	2 Tbsp
1	medium celery root, grated	1
	salt and pepper	

Lentil Salad

An unpretentious salad which may be eaten alone or as a pita filling, garnished with watercress or rocket (for a peppery touch!).

PREPARATION: 15 MIN		4 SERVINGS 200 ML (3/4 CUP)
1	can (540 ml/19 oz) lentils, rinsed and drained	1
3	mini bocconcini, sliced	3
50 ml	red onion, finely chopped	1/4 cup
50 ml	tomatoes, diced	1/4 cup
50 ml	zucchini, diced	1/4 cup
50 ml	red or yellow peppers, diced	1/4 cup
30 ml	oil	2 Tbsp
15 ml	balsamic vinegar	1 Tbsp
10 ml	mint, chopped	2 tsp
45 ml	parsley, chopped	3 Tbsp
	salt and pepper	

Mix all ingredients in a bowl. Salt and pepper to taste.

Tips

Fresh herbs may be replaced with dried herbs using 1/2 the amount.

250 ml (1 cup) dried legumes produces 500-750 ml (2-3 cups) cooked legumes.

Per serving

Calories 262
Sugars 24 g
Protein 17 g
Dietary fibers 4.8 g
Fats 12 g
Sodium 137 mg

Excellent source of folic acid and iron
Good source of magnesium, calcium and fiber
Source of vitamin A, vitamin B12 and vitamin C

Middle-East Salad

This is a typical Lebanese dish where the proportions of the ingredients used will vary according to family traditions. In fact, tabouleh recipes are almost as numerous as the cooks preparing them.

PREPARATION: 15 MIN	COOKING TIME: 5 MIN	5 SERVINGS 300 ML (1 1/4 CUPS)

Tips

When using canned legumes, rinse them well under cold running water. This eliminates at least one third of the added salt to this product, plus some of the sugars responsible for the famous gas!

Tabouleh is more flavorful when it is made a day ahead. For a taste without equal, use fresh parsley, not dried parsley.

Per serving

Calories 251
Sugars 42 g
Protein 10 g
Dietary fiber 4.0 g
Fats 5.8 g
Sodium 206 mg

Excellent source of folic acid and iron
Good source of vitamin C, magnesium and fiber
Source of vitamin A and calcium

In a dutch oven or flame proof casserole, fry the garlic in oil for 2-3 minutes. Add the water and bring to the boil.

Add the seasonings and couscous. Stir and remove from heat.

Cover and let stand 5 minutes.

Using a fork, fluff up the mixture in a large bowl. Incorporate the remaining ingredients.

3	garlic cloves, chopped	3
5 ml	oil	1 tsp
375 ml	water	1 1/2 cups
5 ml	cumin	1 tsp
2 ml	ginger	1/2 tsp
2 ml	turmeric	1/2 tsp
2 ml	chili powder	1/2 tsp
2 ml	salt	1/2 tsp
200 ml	couscous	3/4 cup
45 ml	lemon juice	3 Tbsp
15 ml	mint, chopped or 5 ml (1 tsp) dried mint	1 Tbsp
15 ml	oil	1 Tbsp
2	green onions, chopped	2
1	large tomato, diced	1
200 ml	cucumber, peeled and diced	3/4 cup
375 ml	parsley, chopped	1 1/2 cups
1	can (540 ml/19 oz) chick peas rinsed and drained	1

Tuna Pasta Salad and Sweet Pepper Dressing

This salad offers surprising flavors as well as being an excellent source of vitamin C and iron. In order to obtain higher omega-3 fatty acid content, use albacore tuna.

PREPARATION: 10 MIN	COOKING TIME: 10 MIN	4 SERVINGS 375 ML (1 1/2 CUP)

500 ml	uncooked small pasta	2 cups
1	can (170 g/6 oz) tuna, water packed, drained	1
250 ml	zucchini, diced	1 cup
1	large orange, peeled, removing skin and pith, diced	1
50 ml	red pepper, diced	1/4 cup
50 ml	parsley, chopped or 15 ml (1 Tbsp) dried parsley	1/4 cup
45 ml	red onion, diced	3 Tbsp
200 ml	red pepper dressing	3/4 cup
	(see page 84)	

Cook the pasta in a large pot of salted boiling water until it is *al dente*. Rinse with cold water and set aside.

Mix all the remaining ingredients in a large bowl. Stir in the cooked pasta.

Variation

Replace the tuna with an equal amount of canned shrimp or salmon.

Tip

Got leftover pasta? Drain it and freeze in individual plastic freezer containers. In the morning, add a pasta sauce or one of your favorite toppings and slip it into the lunch box. Reheat it in the microwave for your lunch box meal.

Interesting information

Fish contain omega-3 fatty acids which stimulate the immune system, are an anti-inflammatory and help prevent cancer and heart disease. Nothing better!

Per serving

Calories 308
Sugars 50 g
Protein 17 g
Dietary fiber 3.8 g
Fats 4.2 g
Sodium 25 mg

Excellent source of vitamin B12, vitamin C and iron
Good source of folic acid and magnesium
Source of vitamin A, calcium and fiber

Tortellini Salad with Sun-Dried Tomato Sauce

In spite of its sophisticated appearance, this salad can be made in a jiffy. The sauce will keep refrigerated for up to 2 weeks.

PREPARATION: 15 MIN	COOKING TIME: 10 MIN	4 SERVINGS 375 ML (1 1/2 CUPS)

Tips

Extra virgin olive oil is particularly fine and fruity. It boosts marvelously the flavor of pasta, fries, vegetables, dressings and even bread.

Sun-dried tomato sauce that has been refrigerated, will be easier to mix into tortellini if brought to room temperature first, since cold temperatures thicken olive oil.

This sauce can be used as a spread for bread, in sandwiches, and on fresh chicken, roast beef and pork.

Per serving

Calories 396
Sugars 48 g
Protein 15 g
Dietary fiber 0.2 g
Fats 18 g
Sodium 568 mg

Excellent source of folic acid, magnesium and iron
Good source of vitamin C and calcium
Source of vitamin A and vitamin B12

In a large pot of salted boiling water, cook the tortellini until it is *al dente*. Rinse in cold water and put in a bowl. Add the artichoke hearts and black olives and set aside.

In a food processor, purée all the sauce ingredients.

Incorporate the tortellini and mix gently. Pepper to taste.

---

500 ml	frozen cheese tortellini, uncooked	2 cups
1	can (398 ml/14 oz) artichoke hearts drained and quartered	1
45 ml	black olive slices	3 Tbsp
Sauce		
125 ml	dried tomatoes in oil, drained	1/2 cup
50 ml	extra virgin olive oil	1/4 cup
50 ml	water	1/4 cup
15 ml	basil, chopped or 5 ml (1 tsp) dried basil	1 Tbsp
15 ml	capers	1 Tbsp
15 ml	balsamic vinegar	1 Tbsp
	pepper	

Multi Colored Salad
– Two Methods

Traditional or creamy, your choice...

PREPARATION: 15 MIN		6 SERVINGS 250 ML (1 CUP)

500 ml	green cabbage or fennel, grated	2 cups
500 ml	red cabbage, grated	2 cups
500 ml	carrots, grated	2 cups
15 ml	poppy seeds	1 Tbsp

Mix all the ingredients in a large bowl and set aside.

Creamy Dressing

125 ml	plain yogurt	1/2 cup
75 ml	light mayonnaise	1/3 cup
30 ml	wine vinegar	2 Tbsp
15 ml	hot mustard	1 Tbsp
5 ml	sugar	1 tsp
	salt and pepper	

Creamy Dressing

Mix all the ingredients and incorporate into the salad. Salt and pepper to taste.

Traditional Dressing

50 ml	orange juice	1/4 cup
45 ml	apple cider vinegar	3 Tbsp
45 ml	canola oil	3 Tbsp
10 ml	orange zest	2 tsp
	salt and pepper	

Traditional Dressing

Mix all the ingredients and incorporate into the salad. Salt and pepper to taste.

Tips

This salad is better refrigerated for at least 30 minutes.

Keep poppy seeds refrigerated in an air-tight container, so that they won't go rancid, for up to 6 months.

Per serving

(creamy version)
Calories 94
Sugars 11 g
Protein 2.6 g
Dietary fiber 1.9 g
Fats 5.1 g
Sodium 152 mg

Excellent source of vitamin A
Good source of vitamin C
Source of vitamin B12, folic acid, magnesium, calcium, iron and fiber

Per serving

(traditional version)
Calories 103
Sugars 8.6 g
Protein 1.4 g
Dietary fiber 2.0 g
Fats 7.7 g
Sodium 21 mg

Excellent source of vitamin A and vitamin C
Source of folic acid, magnesium, calcium and fiber

Multi Colored Salad – Two Methods

Tri-Colored Salad

Grilled cauliflower, black beans and sweet red pepper make up this original and nutritious salad!
It keeps well for up to 5 days refrigerated.

PREPARATION: 10 MIN		COOKING TIME: 45 MIN	4 SERVINGS 375 ML (1 1/2 CUPS)

1	cauliflower, cut into florets	1
	oil cooking spray	
50 ml	wine vinegar	1/4 cup
45 ml	olive oil	3 Tbsp
2	large garlic cloves, chopped	2
125 ml	red onion, finely chopped	1/2 cup
2 ml	pepper	1/2 tsp
1 ml	salt	1/2 tsp
45 ml	parsley, chopped or 15 ml (1 Tbsp) dried parsley	3 Tbsp
1	can (540 ml/19 oz) black beans rinsed and drained	1
1	sweet red pepper, diced	1

Preheat the oven to 200°C (400°F).

Spread the cauliflower florets uniformly on an oiled baking sheet. Spray the florets with oil and salt lightly. Cook 45 minutes or just until the cauliflower is golden.

In a large bowl, mix the vinegar, oil, garlic, onion, pepper, salt and parsley. Add the beans and peppers. Mix well and gently fold in the florets.

Tip

Choose a cauliflower that is clean, cream or white colored, firm, compact and without brown blemishes. The leaves should be green and fresh.

Per serving

Calories 271
Sugars 35 g
Protein 12 g
Dietary fiber 7.7 g
Fats 11 g
Sodium 147 mg

Excellent source of folic acid, vitamin C, magnesium and fiber
Good source of iron
Source of vitamin A and calcium

Waldorf Salad

The crunch of apples, celery and red cabbage combined with the velvety dressing makes this salad worthy of the Waldorf Astoria, the prestigious New York hotel after which it is named.

PREPARATION: 15 MIN **4 SERVINGS 375 ML (1 1/2 CUPS)**

Variation
Garnish the salad with a small can (85 g/3 oz) seasoned tuna such as lemon pepper tuna.

Tip
Keep walnuts, almonds, peanuts, pine nuts and other nuts, roasted or natural, refrigerated so they won't go rancid.

Per serving
Calories 143
Sugars 16 g
Protein 1.6 g
Dietary fiber 1.6 g
Fats 3.8 g
Sodium 57 mg

Source of folic acid, vitamin C and magnesium

Put the apples, celery, grapes and red cabbage in a bowl. Sprinkle with lemon juice and mix.

In a small bowl, mix the yogurt, mayonnaise, mustard, honey, chives and celery seed. Salt and pepper to taste.

Pour the dressing on the salad and toss well. Garnish with pecans.

1	McIntosh apple, skin on, cored and cut into fine slices	1
1	Granny Smith apple, skin on, cored, and cut into fine slices	1
1	celery stalk, finely sliced	1
125 ml	green grapes, halved	1/2 cup
200 ml	red cabbage, grated	3/4 cup
15 ml	lemon juice	1 Tbsp
75 ml	plain yogurt	1/3 cup
15 ml	light mayonnaise	1 Tbsp
5 ml	hot mustard	1 tsp
10 ml	honey	2 tsp
15 ml	chives, chopped or 5 ml (1 tsp) dried chives	1 Tbsp
2 ml	celery seed	1/2 tsp
	salt and pepper	
50 ml	pecans or walnuts, roasted and chopped	1/4 cup

Tutti Frutti Salad with Poppy Seed Sauce

A mouth watering delight! This sauce will keep 4 days refrigerated.

PREPARATION: 20 MIN	6 SERVINGS 250 ML (1 CUP)

500 ml	cantaloupe, diced	2 cups
500 ml	honeydew melon, diced	2 cups
250 ml	mango, peeled and diced	1 cup
1	kiwi, peeled and cubed	1

Sauce

200 ml	plain yogurt	3/4 cup
30 ml	concentrated frozen orange juice not diluted	2 Tbsp
15 ml	roasted poppy seeds	1 Tbsp
5 ml	sugar	1 tsp
5 ml	orange zest	1 tsp

Put the fruit in a bowl and toss gently.

Mix all the sauce ingredients until they are homogenous and pour on the fruit.

Variation
For a quick dessert, serve this sauce with a store bought fruit salad! You can also pour it over fresh mixed berries.

Tip
To prepare a mango, cut the fruit in two lengthwise, cutting as close to the pit as possible. Make lattice-like incisions in the flesh, being careful not to cut through to the skin. Turn the skins "inside out" and cut the cubes from the skin.

Nutritional information
The mango is an excellent source of vitamin A and vitamin C. Its flesh is soft, like that of a peach but its taste is spicier.

Per serving
Calories 105
Sugars 22 g
Protein 3.2 g
Dietary fiber 1.8 g
Fats 1.5 g
Sodium 37 mg

Excellent source of vitamin A and vitamin C
Good source of folic acid
Source of vitamin B12, magnesium and calcium
Low in fat

Breads, Pizzas, Sandwiches and Garnishes

Here's to the end of ham and cheese sandwiches! Thanks to the following suggestions, your famished little ones will hurry to see what is hidden between the bread slices … and to sink their teeth into it!

Tuna Wrap

Well wrapped! Here is a sandwich easily eaten ... without leaving crumbs!

PREPARATION: 5 MIN		3 WRAPS
1	can (85 g/3 oz) light tuna flakes with sun-dried tomatoes and basil	1
30 ml	low-fat cream cheese, softened	2 Tbsp
3	tortillas 15 cm (6") in diameter	3
	lettuce leaves	

Blend the tuna and cream cheese until it is homogenized. Spread each tortilla with approximately 30 ml (2 Tbsp) of mixture, garnish with lettuce leaves and roll tightly.

Variations

Use a can of 170 g (6 oz) light flaked tuna in water, well drained, and mix with 50 ml (1/4 cup) cream cheese and 5 ml (1 tsp) dried chives, or with 15 ml (1 Tbsp) remoulade sauce (see page 78). This version makes 6 wraps.

Put cucumber, zucchini, or carrot sticks in the center of the tortilla. Roll up and cut into slices.

Add 50 ml (1/4 cup) grated carrot or zucchini blended with tuna.

Per roll
Calories 116
Sugars 12 g
Protein 11 g
Dietary fiber 1.3 g
Fats 1.3 g
Sodium 124 mg

Excellent source of vitamin B12
Source of magnesium, calcium and iron
Low in fat

Grilled Chicken Sandwich with Caramelized Onions

Main course · Hot/cold

This preparation of chicken and onion can also be used as a hot or cold spread.

PREPARATION: 10 MIN	COOKING TIME: 20 MIN	4 SANDWICHES

5 ml	oil	1 tsp
500 ml	Spanish onion, finely sliced	2 cups
45 ml	sugar	3 Tbsp
30 ml	cider or white vinegar	2 Tbsp
1 ml	thyme	1/4 tsp
4	half chicken breasts, grilled (approx. 300 g/10 oz)	4
15 ml	hot mustard	1 Tbsp
15 ml	light mayonnaise	1 Tbsp
8	slices of light rye bread or 4 ciabatta buns, cut in 2 lengthwise	8

Heat the oil and sauté the onions for 2 minutes. Cover and cook 6 minutes or until they are soft.

Add the sugar, vinegar and thyme. Cook uncovered for 10 minutes, stirring from time to time, until the onions are a light golden color. Set aside.

Spread 4 slices of bread with mustard and mayonnaise. Top with half a chicken breast and garnish with approximately 30 ml (2 Tbsp) caramelized onions. Place the second bread slice on top to complete the sandwiches.

Advance preparation

The caramelized onions can be prepared a day or so ahead. They are equally as delicious served in a hamburger.

Tip

To diminish the vapors that make onions a teary business, place them in the refrigerator for several hours or in the freezer for 20 minutes before cutting them.

Nutritional information

All onions taste sweeter when cooked but certain varieties are naturally sweeter. This is the case with the Spanish onion, which is delicious in relishes, salads and sandwiches.

Per sandwich

Calories 310
Sugars 44 g
Protein 25 g
Dietary fiber 2.8 g
Fats 4.5 g
Sodium 398 mg

Good source of folic acid and magnesium
Source of vitamin B12, vitamin C, calcium, iron and fiber

Quick *Shish Taouk* Sandwich

Main course

Shish taouk lovers will be pleased to find the flavors here that they appreciate so much. This sandwich is delicious served with Middle-East Salad (see page 109).

PREPARATION: 15 MIN	WAITING TIME: 1 HR	COOKING TIME: 25 MIN	6 *shish taouk*

Advance preparation

The chicken can be prepared and cooked up to 3 days ahead.

Tips

Well wrapped in wax paper, sandwiches can be heated in the microwave oven.

Keep several varieties of bread (pitas, tortillas, bagels, sliced or unsliced breads) in the freezer and use just the amount needed at the time.

Per shish taouk

Calories 380
Sugars 45 g
Protein 31 g
Dietary fiber 1.8 g
Fats 8.4 g
Sodium 439 mg

Good source of folic acid and iron
Source of vitamin B12, vitamin C and calcium

Preheat the oven to 190°C (375°F).

Place the chicken in a sealable plastic bag. Add the lemon juice, oil, seasonings and garlic. Close the bag and shake vigorously. Leave it to marinate at least an hour in the refrigerator.

Place the chicken pieces on an oiled baking sheet in the preheated oven for 20 minutes or until the chicken loses its pink color. Cut in strips.

Spread the pitas with hummus and tzatziki. Divide the chicken, onions, tomatoes and cornichons between the 6 pitas and roll them up.

Serve immediately.

500 g	boned chicken breasts	1 lb
30 ml	lemon juice	2 Tbsp
15 ml	oil	1 Tbsp
1 ml	cumin	1/4 tsp
1 ml	coriander	1/4 tsp
1 ml	cinnamon	1/4 tsp
6	large garlic cloves, crushed	6
6	pitas 15 cm (6")	6
125 ml	hummus	1/2 cup
	(commercial brand or see page 74)	
125 ml	tzatziki	1/2 cup
125 ml	red onions, cut in rings	1/2 cup
12	tomato slices	12
3	cornichons (small unsweetened pickled cucumbers), cut lengthwise	3

Chicken and Mango Chutney Sandwich

This sandwich can also be prepared with sliced turkey or pork.

PREPARATION: 10 MIN		4 STUFFED PITAS
250 ml	cooked chicken, in pieces	1 cup
30 ml	mango chutney	2 Tbsp
30 ml	plain yogurt	2 Tbsp
15 ml	light mayonnaise	1 Tbsp
5 ml	dried chives	1 tsp
	lettuce and spinach leaves	
	cucumber slices	
4	whole wheat pitas 15 cm (6")	4

Mix the chicken, chutney, yogurt, mayonnaise and chives until it is a homogenous mixture.

Fill each pita with approximately 75 ml (1/3 cup) of mixture, spinach or lettuce leaves and slices of cucumber.

Variation
Finely chop all the ingredients in a food processor to obtain a spreadable mixture.

Tip
Use frozen bread in sandwich preparation. Fillings spread on it easily and the sandwich bread is kept fresh.

Interesting facts
Chutney is a sweet-sour condiment with a base of cooked fruits or vegetables in vinegar, sugar and spices. It has varying degrees of color pigmentation and has the consistency of jam. The word chutney is taken from the Hindu word "chatni" which means "highly spiced".

Per pita
Calories 275
Sugars 43 g
Protein 20 g
Dietary fiber 4.8 g
Fats 3.8 g
Sodium 405 mg

Good source of magnesium, iron and fiber
Source of vitamin B12 and folic acid

Grilled Apple and Cheese Sandwich

Chicken and Mango Chutney Sandwich   119

Grilled Apple and Cheese Sandwich

Quick · Hot/cold

This sandwich can be eaten hot or cold.

PREPARATION: 10 MIN		1 SANDWICH
2	slices whole wheat bread or walnut bread	2
10 ml	butter or margarine	2tsp
5 ml	hot mustard	1 tsp
2	slices emmenthal cheese approx. 30 g/1 oz)	2
1/2	unpeeled red apple, finely sliced	1/2
	watercress sprigs, shredded lettuce, or alfalfa sprouts	
	mint leaves (optional)	

Butter 2 slices of bread.

Place 1 slice, buttered side down, in a nonstick skillet. Spread the exposed unbuttered side with mustard.

On the bread, place one slice of cheese, the apple slices, a few sprigs of watercress, some mint leaves and the second slice of cheese.

Top the sandwich with a second piece of bread, buttered side up. Fry each side until the bread is golden and the cheese is melted.

Variation

Use roquefort or a cheese containing nuts since these compliment the flavor of the apple. You could replace the apple with a pear.

Tip

Avoid storing crusty breads in plastic bags: the soft interior remains humid while the crust softens. Store it at room temperature, unwrapped. After a day or two, wrap it in a tea towel or put it in a bread box.

Per serving

Calories 361
Sugars 40 g
Protein 14 g
Dietary fiber 4.6 g
Fats 18 g
Sodium 440 mg

Excellent source of vitamin B12 and calcium
Good source of vitamin A, folic acid and fiber
Source of vitamin C, magnesium and iron

Crunchy Cheese Spread

Quick · Vegetarian

Here is a succulent contrast between the cream cheese, the crunch of nuts, and crispness of the apples. This spread can be enjoyed on toast for breakfast, as a mid-day sandwich, or on crackers for an afternoon snack. It keeps 3 days refrigerated.

PREPARATION: 10 MIN   **250 ML (1 CUP)**

Tip
The flavor of nuts is accentuated when they are dry-fried or toasted in a nonstick pan or oven roasted for a few moments until they release their nutty aroma. You can prepare some ahead and freeze until needed.

Per serving
Calories 60
Sugars 3.7 g
Protein 1.9 g
Dietary fiber 0.4 g
Fats 4.6 g
Sodium 106 mg

Source of vitamin A

Combine all ingredients and mix thoroughly.

125 g	low fat cream cheese, softened	4 oz
50 ml	apple, peeled and grated	1/4 cup
50 ml	carrots, grated	1/4 cup
45 ml	toasted nuts	3 Tbsp
30 ml	raisins	2 Tbsp

Pan-Bagnat Sandwich

In Provence, pan-bagnat means "bathed bread" in olive oil.
It refers to the traditional salad niçoise served in a sandwich made with a French baguette.

PREPARATION: 10 MIN		4 PAN-BAGNATS
1	baguette 56 cm (22")	1
30 ml	light mayonnaise	2 Tbsp
10 ml	hot mustard	2 tsp
1	garlic clove, chopped	1
1	can (170 g/6 oz) tuna, water packed, drained	1
45 ml	black olives, chopped	3 Tbsp
3 ml	anchovy paste (optional)	3/4 tsp
1	tomato, diced	1
2	hard cooked eggs, sliced	2
1/2	cucumber, sliced	1/2
	lettuce (mesclun mix)	

Cut the baguette in 4 equal widths, then cut each one in two, lengthwise. Set aside.

In a medium bowl, put the mayonnaise, mustard and garlic. Add tuna, black olives and anchovy paste. Mix tomatoes in gently.

Spread 4 pieces of bread with 50 ml (1/4 cup) tuna mix. Layer on egg and cucumber slices and garnish with mesclun.

Top each piece with the upper slice of bread.

Tip
Sandwiches can be wrapped and stored for 8 hours refrigerated, but the fillings can be kept for 2 days.

Interesting fact
When refrigerated, fresh eggs keep approximately 1 month (check the best-before date on the carton) and hard cooked eggs keep 1 week.

Nutritional information
The mix of salad greens called mesclun (a Provencal word meaning "mix") is made up generally of curly endive, rocket, oak leaf lettuce, radicchio and tender young leaves of escarole and mâche (lambs lettuce). It has a slightly bitter flavor.

Per sandwich
Calories 357
Sugars 49 g
Protein 20 g
Dietary fiber 2.0 g
Fats 7.8 g
Sodium 639 mg

Excellent source of vitamin B12 and iron
Good source of folic acid
Source of vitamin A, vitamin C, magnesium, calcium and fiber

Pan-Bagnat Sandwich

Tomato Parsley

A very versatile spread! Try it on toasted bread, in pasta salad, on grilled chicken, mixed with canned tuna to make a quick sandwich filling, or combined with mayonnaise.

PREPARATION: 10 MIN		**125 ML (1/2 CUP)**
500 ml	parsley	2 cups
2	garlic cloves, chopped	2
15 ml	tomato paste	1 Tbsp
15 ml	white wine vinegar	1 Tbsp
30 ml	extra-virgin olive oil	2 Tbsp

Mix all the ingredients in a food processor. Refrigerate overnight.

Serve at room temperature on toast.

Variation

Mix in 15 ml (1 Tbsp) grated parmesan cheese and 15 ml (1 Tbsp) toasted pine nuts to obtain a parsley pesto.

Per serving (15 ml)

Calories 36
Sugars 1.9 g
Protein 0.5 g
Dietary fiber 0.8 g
Fats 3.3 g
Sodium 6 mg

Source of vitamin A, folic acid, vitamin C and iron

Egg Sandwich

Quick · Vegetarian

This sandwich could be prepared with 3 hard cooked egg whites and 1 hard cooked egg to reduce the cholesterol content.

PREPARATION: 10 MIN   **3 SANDWICHS**

Variations

East Indian style: replace the chives with 2 ml (1/2 tsp) curry powder and a pinch of cayenne.

Mediterranean style: replace the chives and grated carrot with 5 ml (1 tsp) capers and 15 ml (1 Tbsp) chopped parsley. Add 1 ml (1/4 tsp) anchovy paste (optional).

Tip

As soon as eggs are hard cooked, place them in cold water to prevent a dark ring forming around the yolk.

Per sandwich

Calories 270
Sugars 35 g
Protein 12 g
Dietary fiber 4.5 g
Fats 8.9 g
Sodium 532 mg

Excellent source of vitamin A and folic acid
Good source of iron and fiber
Source of magnesium and calcium

Purée eggs in the food processor. Transfer to a small bowl and mix in the yogurt, mayonnaise, grated carrot and chives.

Spread 3 slices of bread with this filling. Garnish with alfalfa sprouts or other greens. Top with remaining slices of bread.

3	hard cooked eggs	3
30 ml	plain yogurt or light sour cream	2 Tbsp
15 ml	light mayonnaise	1 Tbsp
1	small carrot or zucchini, grated	1
15 ml	chives, chopped or 5 ml (1 tsp) dried chives	1 Tbsp
	alfalfa sprouts, small radishes or watercress	
6	slices light rye bread or pumpernickel	6

Roast Beef Emperadado

In Spanish, the word *emperadado* (which comes from *pared*, meaning "wall" or "walled") means "sandwich".

PREPARATION: 10 MIN		3 SANDWICHES	
1	medium avocado, peeled	1	
45 ml	mild salsa	3 Tbsp	
15 ml	butter or margarine	1 Tbsp	
6	slices whole wheat bread or 3 ciabatta buns, cut in half horizontally	6	
125 g	roast beef, sliced	1/4 lb	
	watercress or lettuce		
	tomato slices		

Put the avocado chunks in a small bowl and crush them with a fork. Incorporate the salsa and set aside.

Butter the bread slices to prevent the filling from making the bread soggy.

Spread 3 pieces of bread with the avocado filling. Top with roast beef slices, and garnish with watercress and tomato slices.

Top with remaining bread slices.

Tips
To prepare an avocado, cut it in two lengthwise around the pit, then turn the two halves counter-clockwise to separate. Stick a sharp knife in the pit and turn to detach it.

Freeze leftover roast beef. Partially defrosted, it will shave easily into fine slices for sandwiches or salads.

At the deli counter you can buy sliced plain or seasoned roast beef.

Nutritional information
Avocados are an excellent source of vitamin B6, folic acid and magnesium, as well as monounsaturated fat, a type of fat beneficial to the health of your heart.

Per sandwich
Calories 360
Sugars 33g
Protein 19 g
Dietary fiber 5.7 g
Fats 19 g
Sodium 501 mg

Excellent source of vitamin B12, folic acid, magnesium and iron
Good source of fiber
Source of vitamin A, vitamin C and calcium

Roast Beef Emperadado

Veggie-Burgers

Alone or in a hamburger bun, this preparation, once it is cooked,
could be mistaken for ground beef. However, it is much more flavorful!

PREPARATION: 10 MIN	**COOKING TIME: 20 MIN**	**6 VEGGIE-BURGERS**

10 ml	oil	2 tsp
1	medium onion, chopped	1
3	garlic cloves, chopped	3
8	mushrooms, sliced	8
125 ml	toasted walnuts or pecans	1/2 cup
250 ml	cooked rice	1 cup
250 ml	zucchini, grated	1 cup
250 ml	fresh bread crumbs	1 cup
15 ml	basil, chopped or 5 ml (1 tsp) dried basil	1 Tbsp
1	egg	1
	salt and pepper	

In a skillet, heat oil on medium. Add onion and garlic. Cook, stirring often, for 10 min or until the onion is translucent. Add mushrooms and cook 5 more minutes or until they are soft.

In a food processor, rough chop the nuts. Add the rice, zucchini and cooked vegetables. Mix to obtain a mixture resembling ground beef.

Transfer to a large bowl. Incorporate the bread crumbs, basil and egg. Salt and pepper to taste.

Shape 6 patties approximately 125 ml (1/2 cup) each. Place on an oiled cooking sheet and grill 5-7 minutes each side, until the patties are lightly browned.

Advance preparation
Prepare and shape the patties and freeze them. Cook them as needed.

Nutritional information
Besides being a source of good monounsaturated fats, nuts supply protein, magnesium, zinc, phosphorus, B vitamins and fiber.

Per burger
Calories 170
Sugars 18 g
Protein 4.9 g
Dietary fiber 1.7 g
Fats 9.3 g
Sodium 37 mg

Source of folic acid, vitamin C, magnesium and iron

Italian Quesadillas

Mexican "grilled cheese" loaned to the Italians! Delicious pan fried or oven grilled, hot or cold.
The vegetable filling keeps 3 days refrigerated in an air-tight container.

PREPARATION: 10 MIN   **COOKING TIME: 15 MIN**   **4 QUESADILLAS**

Variation
For an ultra-quick version, use salsa and packaged grated cheese and proceed in the same manner.

Tip
In most recipes, less cheese could be used than indicated, but choose a stronger flavored cheese such as old or extra-old (in this recipe) cheddar, parmesan, blue or emmenthal cheese.

Interesting fact
When cut, plum tomatoes are firm and hold their shape well. If you use another variety, seed it in order to reduce the juice.

Per serving
Calories 271
Sugars 30 g
Protein 11 g
Dietary fiber 3.6 g
Fats 13 g
Sodium 294 mg

Excellent source of vitamin C and calcium
Good source of vitamin A and magnesium
Source of vitamin B12, folic acid, iron and fiber

In a skillet, heat oil and sauté onion, bell pepper and garlic. Cook 10 minutes or until pepper is tender.

Remove from heat, incorporate the tomato, black olives and basil. (This filling of approximately 250 ml/1 cup can be frozen.)

Place 2 tortillas on a work surface. Sprinkle each with approximately 50 ml (1/4 cup) cheese, leaving a border of 2 cm (3/4"). Spread half of the vegetable filling on each tortilla. Sprinkle with remaining cheese. Top with the other 2 tortillas, pressing together gently.

Cook in a nonstick pan 3 minutes. Turn, and cook another 3 minutes or until the cheese is melted and the *quesadillas* are hot.

Cut them in triangles and serve.

5 ml	oil	1 tsp
1	small onion, chopped	1
1	medium red, yellow or green pepper, diced	1
1	garlic clove, diced	1
1	small tomato, diced (Italian plum tomato preferable)	1
30 ml	sliced black olives (optional)	2 Tbsp
2 ml	dried basil	1/2 tsp
4	tortillas 25 cm (10")	4
250 ml	medium cheddar or Monterey Jack, grated	1 cup

Black Olive, Parmesan and Pine Nut Scones

There is nothing like a savory hot scone served with a steaming bowl of soup or red hot chili.

PREPARATION: 10 MIN	**COOKING TIME: 20 MIN**		**9 SCONES**

375	all purpose flour	1 1/2 cups
200 ml	whole wheat flour	3/4 cup
100 ml	parmesan cheese, grated	6 Tbsp
15 ml	baking powder	1 Tbsp
5 ml	dried basil	1 tsp
125 ml	pitted black olives, chopped	1/2 cup
30 ml	toasted pine nuts	2 Tbsp
325 ml	skim milk or buttermilk	1 1/3 cups
	oil	

Preheat oven to 200°C (400°F).

In a large bowl, mix the flours, parmesan cheese, baking powder, basil, olives and pine nuts. Make a well in the center of the dry ingredients and pour in the milk and stir until just moistened.

Using a spoon, drop large dollops of dough (approximately 45 ml/3 Tbsp) on a lightly oiled baking sheet. Spray the scones with a little oil.

Bake 20-25 minutes until the scones are firm to the touch.

Variation
For a totally different flavor, replace black olives with 60 g (2 oz) pancetta (Italian bacon), and parmesan with crumbled gorgonzola (or another blue cheese).

Tip
Do not overmix or the scone dough will become tough.

Per scone
Calories 167
Sugars 28 g
Protein 7.2 g
Dietary fiber 2.6 g
Fats 3.3 g
Sodium 255 mg

Source of vitamin B12, folic acid, magnesium, calcium, iron and fiber

Onion and Gorgonzola Pizza

Simplicity of preparation and quality of the ingredients give this pizza pizzaz "for adults only".

PREPARATION: 20 MIN	COOKING TIME: 5 MIN	6 PIZZA SLICES

Variation

For an even more surprising flavor, replace the onion with two pears, finely sliced, and omit the basil.

Interesting fact

In the flavorful world of blue cheese, gorgonzola is as well known in Italy as roquefort is in France, and stilton is in England. Its flavor is rich, with a sharp, slightly peppery taste.

Per slice

Calories 244
Sugars 27 g
Protein 9.7 g
Dietary fiber 1.7 g
Fats 11 g
Sodium 461 mg

Good source of iron
Source of vitamin B12, folic acid, vitamin C, magnesium and calcium

Preheat oven to 200°C (400°F).

Sauté onions in oil until they are golden, approximately 15 minutes. (If they stick, add a few spoonfuls of water and continue cooking.) Spread onions on the pizza crust. Garnish with crumbled gorgonzola, basil leaves and pine nuts. Pepper to taste.

Bake 5 minutes or just until the pizza is golden.

500 ml	Spanish onion, finely sliced	2 cups
15 ml	oil	1 Tbsp
1	thin pizza crust 25 cm (10") diameter	1
100 g	gorgonzola, crumbled	3 oz
	basil leaves	
45 ml	toasted pine nuts	3 Tbsp
	pepper	

Pizza Pockets

This recipe wins hands down over commercially made pizza for its flavor, nutritive value and cost. And delivery is free!

PREPARATION: 15 MIN		COOKING TIME: 10 MIN	6 POCKETS

5 ml	oil	1 tsp
1	small onion, finely sliced	1
375 ml	mushrooms, sliced	1 1/2 cups
15 ml	dried tomatoes, rehydrated and chopped	1 Tbsp
6	wheat tortillas 5 cm (10") in diameter	6
1	can (213 ml/7.5 oz) pizza sauce	1
20	slices vegetarian pizza pepperoni	20
250 ml	low fat mozzarella, grated	1 cup

Preheat oven to 200°C (400°F).

In a nonstick skillet, heat oil and sauté onions, mushrooms and rehydrated dried tomatoes until onions are transparent.

Place the tortillas on a work surface and spread with pizza sauce. Place the vegetable mixture, pepperoni slices and mozzarella, in the center of each tortilla.

Form a pocket by folding the bottom edge over the filling, then folding in each side and finally the top edge. Place the pockets, folded side down, on a baking sheet. Bake for 10 minutes or until the pockets are hot.

In a microwave, each pocket will take approximately 30 seconds on high.

Variation
For variety, use pesto, herb, or dried tomato tortillas.

Interesting fact
One commercially made pizza pocket (approximately 100 g/3 oz, the equivalent of "only" 1/8th of a pizza 30 cm/12") in diameter), supplies as much fat as two pats of butter and 20% of the daily recommended amount of salt.

Nutritional information
In the grocery store, you can find soy pepperoni, sausage, bacon and other soy based products. This is one way to cut down on hidden saturated fat, cholesterol and sodium in ready-made foods.

Per serving
Calories 219
Sugars 30 g
Protein 12 g
Dietary fiber 3.6 g
Fats 6.2 g
Sodium 422 mg

Good source of vitamin B12, magnesium and calcium
Source of vitamin A, folic acid, vitamin C, iron and fiber

Eggs and Pasta

These foods are easy to digest, nutritious, versatile, economical, and are taste bud pleasers for people of any age. Each is worth making as a main course!

Kiddies Confetti Rice

Quick · Vegetarian · Hot/cold

An unpretentious dish, quick and nutritious, that the children can make themselves!

PREPARATION: 5 MIN		COOKING TIME: 5 MIN	4 SERVINGS

250 ml	cooked brown rice	1 cup
3	eggs	3
1	green onion, finely chopped	1
30 ml	red bell pepper, diced	2 Tbsp
30 ml	cooked kernel corn or green peas	2 Tbsp
30 ml	milk	2 Tbsp
5 ml	dried parsley	1 tsp
45 ml	low fat mozzarella, grated	3 Tbsp
5 ml	hot mustard	1 tsp
	salt and pepper	

Mix all ingredients in a bowl. Salt and pepper to taste.

Divide the mixture between 4 microwave-proof ramekins 125 ml (1/2 cup).

In microwave, cook on high 4-6 minutes or until the custard has set. If cooking individually, cook 1 1/2 minutes on high.

Let cool for a moment before turning out on a plate. Serve immediately.

Tips

Leave fresh eggs in their egg carton to protect them from odors. Do not store them in the refrigerator door because the temperature is colder there.

When reheating food in the microwave, use only microwave-proof plastic containers where it is clearly stated on the label.

Nutritional information

Eggs provide good nutrition and are low in calories. It doesn't matter if they are brown or white: the color of the shell is dictated by the breed of chicken and does not affect its taste or nutritional value.

Per serving

Calories 138
Sugars 14 g
Protein 8.0 g
Dietary fiber 1.1 g
Fats 5.3 g
Sodium 99 mg

Good source of vitamin B12
Source of vitamin A, folic acid, vitamin C, magnesium, calcium and iron

Kiddies Confetti Rice

Forestière Quiche

Can be frozen · Vegetarian · Hot/cold

A memorable quiche, especially with a crisp salad!
Here is a dish which is prepared with no fuss, no muss.

PREPARATION: 15 MIN		COOKING TIME: 50 MIN	6 SERVING

10 ml	oil	2 tsp
500 ml	leeks, chopped	2 cups
250 ml	mushrooms, sliced	1 cup
1	pastry shell 23 cm (9") diameter, uncooked	1
1	container (250 g/1/2 lb) 1% cottage cheese	1
3	eggs, beaten	3
100 ml	milk	6 Tbsp
2 ml	salt	1/2 tsp
1 ml	pepper	1/4 tsp
15 ml	chives, chopped or 5 ml (1 tsp) dried chives	1 Tbsp

Preheat oven to 190°C (375°F).

In a small skillet, heat oil on medium. Add leeks and mushrooms and cook, stirring occasionally, for approximately 10 minutes or until cooking liquid has evaporated.

Place uncooked pastry shell in quiche dish. Spread vegetables evenly over the pastry and set aside.

In a bowl, mix cottage cheese, eggs, milk, salt, pepper and chives. Pour over the vegetables.

Place the quiche dish on a baking sheet and cook 50-55 minutes or until the top is golden.

Advance preparation

Prepare two quiches at a time. Eat one the same day and freeze the second one for a later date.

Tips

When cooking the pastry dough in an aluminum pie plate, place the pie plate on a baking sheet. The bottom will be golden and well cooked.

Prepare this quiche without the crust and cut out 150 calories and 10 g fat per serving. Don't forget to oil the quiche dish well.

The use of cottage cheese in this recipe supplies a little more calcium, reduces the use of eggs and contributes to its texture.

Per serving

Calories 263
Sugars 21 g
Protein 12 g
Dietary fiber 1.1 g
Fats 15 g
Sodium 566 mg

Excellent source of vitamin B12
Good source of folic acid
Source of vitamin A, vitamin C, magnesium, calcium and iron

Spanish Tortilla

Viva Espana! This flavorful omelet is prepared in a jiffy!

PREPARATION: 10 MIN	COOKING TIME: 15 MIN	4 SERVINGS

Tips

This tortilla can be heated in the microwave. It is also delicious served cold.

If the handle of your skillet is made of wood or plastic, wrap it in aluminum foil to protect it from the heat of the oven.

Interesting fact

In Spanish, the word tortilla means "cookie". A Spanish omelet is always made with a mix of eggs and potatoes.

Per serving

Calories 199
Sugars 21 g
Protein 10 g
Dietary fiber 2.2 g
Fats 8.7 g
Sodium 85 mg

Excellent source of vitamin B12 and vitamin C
Good source of vitamin A and folic acid
Source of magnesium, iron and fiber

Heat oil on medium in a nonstick skillet and add all the vegetables. Cover and let cook 10 minutes or just until the potatoes are tender. Salt and pepper to taste.

In a bowl, beat eggs with a fork. Add the Tabasco.

Pour the egg mixture on the vegetables and cook on medium for 5 minutes or until the bottom of the omelet is golden.

The omelet may be placed under the broiler for 2-3 minutes until the top is golden.

10 ml	oil	2 tsp
2	small potatoes, peeled and finely sliced	2
1	small onion, sliced very thin	1
1/2	red bell pepper	1/2
1	can (199 ml/7oz) kernel corn, drained	1
	salt and pepper	
5	eggs	5
	a few drops Tabasco	

137

Artichoke and Parmesan Frittata

The frittata, an Italian omelet, is prepared with vegetables and grilled on both sides. It can be prepared the day before and eaten hot or cold.

PREPARATION: 5 MIN		COOKING TIME: 10 MIN	5 SERVINGS

10 ml	oil	2 tsp
1	medium onion, finely chopped	1
1	garlic clove, finely chopped	1
1	can (398 ml/14 oz) artichoke hearts, quartered	1
4	eggs	4
50 ml	parmesan cheese, grated	1/4 cup
5 ml	oregano	1 tsp
1 ml	pepper	1/4 tsp

Heat oil on medium in a nonstick skillet, and sauté the onions 5 minutes or until they are transparent. Add the garlic and cook 1 minute. Add the artichokes and heat. Spread the vegetables evenly in the bottom of the skillet.

In a bowl, beat the eggs with a fork, along with the parmesan cheese, oregano and pepper. Pour egg mixture on the vegetables and cook on medium 10 minutes or until the bottom of the omelet is golden.

You can also put the skillet under the broiler until the top is golden. Serve.

Tip

This frittata reheats well in the microwave oven. It can also be served cold with a green salad and a slice of whole wheat bread.

Nutritional information

In most recipes (cakes, muffins, omelets and quiches), 1 or 2 whole eggs may be replaced with egg whites: 2 egg whites replace 1 whole egg.

Per serving

Calories 165
Sugars 17 g
Protein 11 g
Dietary fiber 0.6 g
Fats 7.1 g
Sodium 228 mg

Excellent source of folic acid and magnesium
Good source of vitamin B12 and iron
Source of vitamin A, vitamin C, and calcium

Artichoke and Parmesan Frittata

Italian Pasta Omelet

This new type of omelet is an ideal way to "recycle" leftover spaghetti. It can be easily prepared the day before.

PREPARATION: 5 MIN		**COOKING TIME: 20 MIN**	**5 SERVINGS**

10 ml	oil	2 tsp
1	small onion, chopped	1
375 ml	mushrooms, sliced	1 1/2 cup
	salt and pepper	
6	eggs	6
15 ml	pesto or tomato parsley (see page 124)	1 Tbsp
45 ml	parmesan cheese, grated	3 Tbsp
15 ml	parsley, chopped	1 Tbsp
500 ml	cooked pasta (spaghetti, angel hair)	2 cups

Quick Tomato Sauce

5 ml	oil	1 tsp
1	garlic clove, chopped	1
1	can (213 ml/7.5 oz) tomato sauce	1
5 ml	sugar	1 tsp
1	pinch dried chili pepper flakes	1
	salt and pepper	

Heat oil on medium in a nonstick skillet. Sauté onions and mushrooms, stirring occasionally, for 10 minutes or until cooking liquid has evaporated. Salt and pepper to taste.

In a bowl, beat the eggs, pesto, parmesan cheese and parsley with a fork. Incorporate the noodles.

Pour egg mixture on the vegetables and cook on high for 4 minutes. Lower heat and cook on medium until the bottom of the omelet is golden.

The omelet may be grilled under the broiler for a few moments until golden. Serve hot or cold with tomato sauce.

Quick Tomato Sauce
In a small heavy-bottom pot, heat oil and sauté the garlic without browning it. Add tomato sauce, chili flakes and sugar. Let simmer 10 minutes. Salt and pepper to taste.

Tip
For quick hard cooked eggs, use the microwave oven. Break an egg into an oiled ramekin, prick the egg yolk, cover with a sheet of plastic wrap, lifting one corner of wrap, and cook at medium heat 1 to 1 1/2 minutes or until the yolk is firm. Let rest 5 minutes. Never try to cook an egg in its shell in the microwave oven.

Nutritional information
For less cholesterol, use a blend of egg whites and commercial pasteurized liquid eggs. Replace 1 or 2 whole eggs with egg whites, using 2 egg whites per whole egg.

Per serving
(with tomato sauce)
Calories 261
Sugars 26 g
Protein 13 g
Dietary fiber 2.5 g
Fats 12 g
Sodium 410 mg

Excellent source of vitamin B12
Good source of vitamin A, folic acid and iron
Source of vitamin C, magnesium, calcium and fiber

Alfre-Tofu Fettuccini

Pasta, and more pasta! The kids will love its sweet sauce, and so will parents for its nutritive value!

PREPARATION: 5 MIN	COOKING TIME: 15 MIN	4 SERVINGS 375 ML (1 1/2 CUP)

Variation

For a rose sauce add 30 ml (2 Tbsp) tomato paste to the tofu mixture.

Interesting fact

Fresh tofu is a lovely cream color and is almost odorless. Its texture is smooth, not sticky, and firm but elastic.

Nutritional information

The pastas which have "enriched" mentioned on the label have had additions of iron and the four B vitamins (folic acid, thiamin, riboflavin and niacin). For white pasta lovers, it is the one to choose.

Per serving

Calories 375
Sugars 64 g
Protein 16 g
Dietary fiber 3.7 g
Fats 5.7 g
Sodium 302 mg

Excellent source of magnesium and iron
Source of vitamin B12, folic acid, calcium and fiber

In a bowl, using a hand mixer, blend the tofu to a purée with the milk. Stir in the basil, oregano and salt and set aside.

In a large skillet, sauté onions in oil for 5 minutes without browning them. Add the tofu and milk mixture and simmer a few minutes until the sauce is hot. Pepper to taste.

Meanwhile, cook the fettuccini *al dente*. Drain and stir in the sauce. Sprinkle with parmesan and serve immediately.

1	pack (300 g/10 oz) soft tofu	1
125 ml	milk	1/2 cup
5 ml	dried basil	1 tsp
5 ml	oregano	1 tsp
2 ml	salt	1/2 tsp
5 ml	oil	1 tsp
3	garlic cloves, chopped	3
30 ml	parmesan cheese, grated	2 Tbsp
	pepper	
350 g	fettuccini, uncooked	12 oz
	parmesan cheese, grated	

Macaroni and Cheese "Secret Code"

Quick • Vegetarian

The secret code is almost impossible to detect: this sauce has a tofu base!

| PREPARATION: 5 MIN | COOKING TIME: 10 MIN | 5 SERVINGS 300 ML (1 1/4 CUPS) |

1	pkg (225 g/1/2 lb) macaroni and cheese	1
250 ml	fusilli, uncooked	1 cup
250 ml	frozen green peas or broccoli florets	1 cup
1	pack (300 g/10 oz) soft tofu	1
30 ml	chives, chopped or 10 ml (2 tsp) dried chives	2 Tbsp
	pepper	

Cook the macaroni and fusilli in boiling, salted water. A few minutes before the end of the cooking time, add peas or broccoli, then continue to cook. Drain and set aside.

Meanwhile, purée the tofu using a hand mixer. Incorporate the small bag of cheese sauce contained in the macaroni and cheese box and also the chives.

Pour the tofu mixture on the cooked noodles, mix and pepper to taste. Serve immediately.

Interesting fact

Tofu is made from soy milk to which a coagulant is added to form curds, a process much the same as in making cheese. Firm or extra-firm tofu can be sautéed, grilled or poached in a soup but soft tofu cannot. It is ideal incorporated in a homogenous sweet or salted mixture.

Nutritional information

Adding tofu and extra pasta enriches the commercial product and dilutes the salt content, often high, in these processed foods.

Per serving

Calories 241
Sugars 36 g
Protein 12 g
Dietary fiber 2.3 g
Fats 5.4 g
Sodium 326 mg

Good source of magnesium and iron
Source of vitamin A, vitamin B12, folic acid, vitamin C, calcium and fiber

Macaroni with all the trimmings!

This macaroni will convince the meat substitute skeptics!
At least if you don't tell them the ingredients...

PREPARATION: 15 MIN	**COOKING TIME: 20 MIN**	**5 SERVINGS 375 ML (1 1/2 CUPS)**

Variation
Add a can (540 ml/19 oz) of red kidney beans, rinsed, to make this a chili macaroni with all the trimmings!

Tip
The veggie ground round produces a better result if it is added, crumbled, at the end of cooking.

Interesting facts
Veggie ground round has the same texture as ground beef while containing much less fat and the same quantity of protein. A package of 340 g contains the equivalent of 680 g cooked ground beef or 1 kg (2 lbs) raw ground beef.

Per serving
Calories 199
Sugars 29 g
Protein 18 g
Dietary fiber 3.3 g
Fats 2.0 g
Sodium 558 mg

Excellent source of vitamin A
Good source of vitamin C and iron
Source of vitamin B12, folic acid, magnesium, calcium and fiber
Low in fat

In a large saucepan, heat oil and sauté the onions, garlic and carrots for 5 minutes or until onions are tender.

Stir in the tomatoes, chili, cumin, oregano and chili flakes. Bring to the boil, lower the heat and simmer 15 minutes.

Meanwhile, cook the macaroni until it is *al dente*. Incorporate lemon juice, cooked macaroni, veggie ground round, coriander and salt into the above mixture. Pepper to taste.

Add water if the mixture is too thick.

5 ml	oil	1 tsp
1	large onion, chopped	1
2	garlic cloves, chopped	2
1	large carrot, diced	1
1	can (796 ml/28 oz) diced tomatoes	1
15 ml	chili powder	1 Tbsp
5 ml	cumin	1 tsp
5 ml	oregano	1 tsp
1 ml	chili pepper flakes	1/4 tsp
250 ml	macaroni, uncooked	1 cup
15 ml	lemon or lime juice	1 Tbsp
1	pkg (340 g/12 oz) veggie ground round	
45 ml	coriander or parsley, chopped or 15 ml (1 tsp) dried parsley	3 Tbsp
2 ml	salt	1/2 tsp
	pepper	

143

Mamma Mia Polenta

A little taste of Italy that you will quickly adopt.

10 ml	oil	2 tsp
1	onion, chopped	1
1	garlic clove, chopped	1
1	green pepper, diced	1
8	mushrooms, sliced	8
1	can (796 ml/28 oz) diced tomatoes	1
45 ml	parsley, chopped or 15 ml (1 Tbsp) dried parsley	3 Tbsp
15 ml	basil, chopped or 5 ml (1 tsp) dried basil	1 Tbsp
2 ml	salt	1/2 tsp
	a few drops Tabasco	
5	mild or spicy Italian sausages cut in 2 cm (3/4") slices	5
1	pkg (500 g/1 lb) prepared polenta	1
125 ml	low fat mozzarella, grated	1/2 cup
	parmesan cheese	

Preheat oven to 180°C (350°F).

In a large saucepan, heat the oil and sauté onion and garlic until tender. Add green pepper and mushrooms and cook 5 more minutes. Add tomatoes and seasonings and simmer 20 minutes longer.

Meanwhile, sauté the sausage slices in a non-stick skillet until they are lightly browned.

Cut the "sausage" of polenta in 1 cm (1/2") thick slices and place them in a uniform layer in a 3 L (12 cup) heat-proof casserole dish.

As soon as the sausages are browned, stir them into the sauce and pour it over the polenta. Sprinkle with grated mozzarella and parmesan cheese.

Bake in the oven 15 minutes or until cheese is melted.

Tip
For a quick recipe, use a can (700 ml/26 oz) of tomato sauce such as primavera, mushroom or zucchini.

Interesting fact
Polenta, made from cornmeal, is of Italian peasant origin, especially popular in Northern Italy, substituting for pasta and bread. It is cut into slices and grilled under the broiler or fried in oil and served as an accompaniment to parmesan cheese or a sauce. Polenta can also be purchased ready-made.

Per serving
Calories 279 g
Sugars 25 g
Protein 14 g
Dietary fiber 2.3 g
Fats 14 g
Sodium 798 mg

Excellent source of vitamin B12
Good source of vitamin C
Source of vitamin A, folic acid, magnesium, calcium, iron and fiber

Mamma Mia Polenta

Cheese and Onion Pasta

Here is a dish which will please the children as well as the adults.

PREPARATION: 15 MIN	COOKING TIME: 15 MIN	6 SERVINGS 300 ML (1 1/4 CUPS)

750 ml	pasta shells or fusilli, uncooked	3 cups
10 ml	oil	2 tsp
1	medium onion, chopped	1
2	green onions, chopped	2
375 ml	mushrooms, sliced	1 1/2 cups
75 ml	flour	1/3 cup
650 ml	hot milk	2 2/3 cups
50 ml	chives, chopped or 15 ml (1 Tbsp) dried chives	1/4 cup
100 g	spreadable processed cheese product	3 oz
125 ml	extra-old cheddar cheese	1/2 cup
125 ml	parmesan cheese, grated	1/2 cup
	pepper	

Cook pasta in boiling salted water. Meanwhile, heat oil in a skillet and sauté the onion, green onions and mushrooms until the onion is transparent. Set aside.

Put flour in a large saucepan. Add hot milk and cook on medium heat while whipping constantly with a whisk for 5 minutes, or until the sauce thickens. Add the chives, cheeses and vegetable mixture. As soon as the cheeses are melted, pepper to taste and add the pasta.

Variation
Incorporate cooked vegetables such as broccoli florets, sliced carrots or green peas. For a different flavor while adding additional protein, stir in canned tuna.

Tip
When reheating pasta add a little milk, stirring well, since the sauce thickens when chilled.

Nutritional information
250 ml (1 cup) cooked whole wheat pasta supplies 6.3 g fiber whereas the same amount of white pasta supplies 2.4 g fiber. This is nearly triple for almost an identical taste.

Per serving
Calories 471
Sugars 65 g
Protein 24 g
Dietary fiber 3.8 g
Fats 12 g
Sodium 580 mg

Excellent source of vitamin B12, magnesium, calcium and iron
Good source of vitamin A and folic acid
Source of vitamin C and fiber

Chicken and Beef

Eat beef. It is permitted! Be wise and leave the larger portion of the plate for vegetables, salad and legumes.

Lebanese Samosas

Hot, hot pockets! These take as little time to prepare as to eat!

PREPARATION: 20 MIN	COOKING TIME: 20 MIN	25 SAMOSAS

5 ml	oil	1 tsp
250 g	lean ground beef	1/2 lb
1	medium onion, finely sliced	1
20 ml	fresh ginger, finely chopped	4 tsp
10 ml	cumin	2 tsp
3 ml	turmeric	3/4 tsp
1	medium potato, peeled and diced	1
200 ml	frozen green peas	3/4 cup
200 ml	water	3/4 cup
45 ml	toasted pine nuts	3 Tbsp
1	pkg (454 g/1 lb) egg roll	1
	pastry squares	
	salt and pepper	
1	egg, lightly beaten	1
	sour cream	

Preheat oven to 200°C (400°F).

Heat oil in a skillet and sauté the beef, onion, ginger, cumin and turmeric just until the beef is browned. Add potato, peas and water. Cover and cook 10 minutes or until the potatoes are cooked and there is no liquid.

Transfer to a bowl and stir in the pine nuts and let cool.

Place 15 ml (1 Tbsp) meat mixture on each sheet of pastry. Fold the pastry to form a triangle and brush with a little beaten egg. Continue until the stuffing is finished, producing approximately 25 samosas.

Place on an oiled or parchment covered baking sheet. Oil or spray oil on two sides of the samosas. Bake for 10 minutes in oven. Turn the samosas and bake for 10 minutes more or until they are golden.

Serve hot with sour cream.

Advance preparation
The meat may be prepared up to 2 days ahead and stored in either the refrigerator or freezer. The samosas can be frozen, and then cooked when desired.

Per serving of 3 samosas
Calories 254
Sugars 37 g
Protein 13 g
Dietary fiber 1.7 g
Fats 6.1 g
Sodium 189 mg

Excellent source of vitamin B
Source of folic acid, vitamin C, magnesium and iron

Crusty Chicken Nuggets

Crusty Chicken Nuggets

These chicken nuggets don't need to be fried in oil to be crusty. They are delicious served with sweet and sour sauce (see page 77). The children will ask for more!

PREPARATION: 10 MIN	COOKING TIME: 15 MIN	8 SERVINGS

500 ml	corn flakes	2 cups
200 ml	plain or roasted peanuts	3/4 cup
5 ml	onion salt	1 tsp
200 ml	milk	3/4 cup
45 ml	plain yogurt or sour cream	3 Tbsp
750 g	chicken breast, cut in bite-size pieces	1 1/2 lb

Preheat oven to 220°C (425°F).

In a food processor, reduce the corn flakes to fine crumbs. Place in a deep dish.

In a food processor, pulse the peanuts into a coarse chop. Mix with cornflake crumbs. Add onion salt.

Dip chicken pieces in the milk and yogurt mixture (if time allows, leave them to marinate several hours and then drain).

Roll chicken pieces in the corn flake mixture. Place them on a lightly oiled baking sheet. Cook for 15 minutes.

Serve hot or warm.

Advance preparation
Make the crumb dressing mixture a day ahead. It can also be frozen.

Variation
For a more "adult" taste, add chili pepper flakes, curry or chili powder.

Interesting fact
Peanuts are not a nut but a legume belonging to the same family as dried peas and beans. They grow underground: as soon as the flowers are fertilized, they wilt and the stems arc toward the ground and root in the earth to give birth to the peanut!

Per serving
Calories 252
Sugars 12 g
Protein 30 g
Dietary fiber 1.4 g
Fats 9.5 g
Sodium 147 mg

Good source of vitamin B12 and magnesium
Source of folic acid, calcium and iron

Quick Egg Rolls

Can be frozen

You will appreciate these for lunches and quick meals. They can be heated in the oven or fried.

PREPARATION: 15 MIN	COOKING TIME: 20 MIN	25 EGG ROLLS

Advance preparation

Prepare the meat stuffing in advance and refrigerate for up to 2 days, or freeze it. Egg rolls can be prepared and frozen, cooked or uncooked.

Nutritional information

Ground chicken is very perishable. Use it the same day or freeze it. If you have a food processor, make your own ground meat from skinless and boneless chicken breasts for a lean and fresh product.

Per serving

Calories 195
Sugars 33 g
Protein 12 g
Dietary fiber 0.1 g
Fats 1.5 g
Sodium 309 mg

Good source of vitamin C
Source of vitamin A and vitamin B12
Low in fat

Preheat oven to 200°C (400°F).

Heat oil in a skillet. Sauté all ingredients, except egg roll pastry squares, until the meat is browned. Let cool.

Place approximately 15 ml (1 Tbsp) filling on each pastry square. Fold to form a rectangle and seal with a little of the egg wash. Proceed in this manner until all the filling is used to make approximately 25 egg rolls.

Place them on an oiled or parchment lined baking sheet. Spray or brush oil on both sides of the egg rolls. Cook in oven for 10 minutes.

Turn the egg rolls and cook 10 minutes longer until they are golden.

5 ml	oil	1 tsp
250 g	lean ground chicken or veal	1/2 lb
150 ml	shredded green cabbage	1/2 cup
1	small red bell pepper, diced	1
2	green onions, chopped	2
2	garlic cloves, chopped	2
45 ml	chili sauce	3 Tbsp
15 ml	peeled ginger, finely chopped	1 Tbsp
15 ml	soy sauce	1 Tbsp
1	pkg (454 g/1 lb) egg roll pastry squares	1
1	egg, lightly beaten (egg wash)	1
	oil cooking spray	

Oriental Chicken Stir-fry

Let's stir-fry! Here is a way to transform leftover vegetables into a unique, flavorful dish. Best yet, the rapid cooking of the vegetables conserve a good part of their nutritional value.

| PREPARATION: 15 MIN | | COOKING TIME: 15 MIN | | 6 SERVINGS 300 ML (1 1/4 CUPS) |

15 ml	corn starch	1 Tbsp
15 ml	soy sauce	1 Tbsp
400 g	chicken breasts	14 oz
15 ml	oil	1 Tbsp
3	garlic cloves, finely chopped	3
15 ml	peeled ginger, finely chopped	1 Tbsp
2	green onions, chopped	2
1	large onion, chopped	1
500 ml	broccoli florets	2 cups
500 ml	cauliflower florets	2 cups
250 ml	carrots, sliced	1 cup
50 ml	orange juice	1/4 cup
1	can (284 ml/10 oz) mandarin oranges drained	1
	salt, pepper and sesame seeds	

Sauce

150 ml	chicken bouillon	2/3 cup
15 ml	light soy sauce	1 Tbsp
15 ml	sesame seeds	1 Tbsp
15 ml	corn starch	1 Tbsp
5 ml	sesame oil	1 tsp
	red chili flakes	

In a large bowl, stir the corn starch into the soy sauce and marinate the chicken in this mixture.

In another bowl, mix all the sauce ingredients and set aside.

Heat oil in a wok or a large deep skillet. Cook garlic, ginger, green onions and onion for 1 minute.

Add marinated chicken and cook just until it is lightly golden. Add broccoli, cauliflower, carrots and orange juice. Cover and cook 3-5 minutes until the flesh of the chicken is no longer pink. Add the mandarin sections.

Mix the sauce well. Incorporate it into the chicken mixture and cook for several minutes. Salt and pepper to taste and sprinkle with sesame seeds.

Serve on a nest of basmati rice or rice vermicelli.

Variation

For a Thai taste, add 30 ml (2 Tbsp) coconut milk and 45 ml (3 Tbsp) peanut butter to the sauce.

Tip

To have the vegetables cook evenly, cut them the same size. Begin by cooking firm vegetables first such as the broccoli, cauliflower and carrots, before the more tender vegetables such as mushrooms, peppers or zucchini. The wok should be very hot in order to achieve a fast cooking time.

Per serving

Calories 179
Sugars 13 g
Protein 20 g
Dietary fiber 2.2 g
Fats 5.2 g
Sodium 404 mg

Excellent source of vitamin A and vitamin C
Good source of folic acid and magnesium
Source of vitamin B12, iron and fiber

Moroccan Fruit Casserole

Main dish · Can be frozen

This tastes even better reheated the next day. Serve with couscous.

PREPARATION: 20 MIN **COOKING TIME: 60 MIN** **8 SERVINGS**

Interesting fact
A serving of meat equaling the size of a pack of playing cards supplies an ample serving of protein. Accompany the protein with a profusion of vegetables, fruit and a grain such as in this recipe, to obtain a wide variety of nutrients.

Nutritional information
The more orange it is, the deeper the color, the higher the beta-carotene pigment which transforms into vitamin A in the body. The carrots and sweet potatoes, the base of this recipe, are excellent sources of this vitamin, friend to the bones, eyes and skin.

Per serving
Calories 383
Sugars 40 g
Protein 30 g
Dietary fiber 5.0 g
Fats 12 g
Sodium 304 mg

Excellent source of vitamin A, vitamin B12, and iron
Good source of vitamin C, magnesium and fiber
Source of folic acid and calcium

Preheat oven to 180°C (350°F).

In a large saucepan, sauté meat in oil on high, a small amount at a time, to braise well. Set aside. Lower heat to medium and sauté onions, garlic, carrots and sweet potato until the vegetables are tender, approximately 4 minutes.

Add apple and seasonings. Cook 2 minutes.

Put meat in the saucepan, mix in the dry fruits, tomato, water and apple juice. Cover and cook in oven for 60 minutes or until the meat is tender.

1 kg	lean beef, cut into equal sized cubes	2 lb
15 ml	oil	1 Tbsp
2	medium onions, chopped coarsely	2
2	garlic cloves, chopped	2
2	carrots, sliced	2
1	sweet potato, peeled and diced	1
1	apple, peeled and diced	1
2 ml	ginger	1/2 tsp
2 ml	curry	1/2 tsp
2 ml	cinnamon	1/2 tsp
2 ml	salt	1/2 tsp
12	dried apricots, cut into matchsticks	12
12	prunes, pitted and cut in two	12
12	dates, pitted and cut in two	12
50 ml	raisins	1/4 cup
1	can (540 ml/19 oz) diced tomatoes	1
250 ml	water	1 cup
125 ml	apple juice or white wine	1/2 cup

Québécois Shepherd's Pie

Here is Isabelle's family's shepherd's pie. According to the inspiration of the moment (and the contents of the refrigerator!), she adds a few mushrooms, diced zucchini or even grated carrot and cooked onion.

PREPARATION: 25 MIN   **COOKING TIME: 30 MIN**   **9 SERVINGS**

4	large potatoes, peeled	4
2	large carrots, thickly sliced	2
30 ml	parmesan cheese, grated	2 Tbsp
30 ml	milk	2 Tbsp
15 ml	chives, chopped or 5 ml (1 tsp) dried chives	1 Tbsp
5 ml	oil	1 tsp
1	onion or leek, chopped	1
1	pkg (300 g/10 oz) frozen spinach chopped	1
500 g	lean ground beef	1 lb
15 ml	Worcestershire sauce	1 Tbsp
5 ml	herbs de Provence	1 tsp
	pepper	
1	can (398 ml/14 oz) cream corn	1
1	can (199 ml/7 oz) kernel corn, drained	1

Preheat oven to 180°C (350°F).

In a saucepan of salted, boiling water, cook potatoes and carrots until tender, drain. Purée, using a hand blender. Stir in parmesan cheese, milk and chives. Set aside.

In a skillet, heat oil and sauté onion about 5 minutes just until it is translucent. Add spinach and cook until it is defrosted and liquid is evaporated. Put spinach in a heat proof 3 L (12 cup) casserole dish.

In the same skillet, brown meat and drain off any liquids. Add the Worcestershire sauce, herbs de Provence, and pepper to taste. Stir into the cooked spinach mixture in casserole dish. Layer the creamed and kernel corn, then top with the puréed potatoes and carrots. Cook 30 minutes in the oven or until the casserole is hot and slightly golden on top.

Variation

Replace some or all of the ground beef with veggie ground round. This protein substitute is based on soy and wheat protein and contains no fat or cholesterol, and is approximately half the price of lean ground beef.

Interesting facts

Herbs de Provence is composed of a blend of equal amounts of rosemary, sage, basil and savory.

By draining off the rendered fat from the cooked beef before adding the other ingredients of this recipe, it reduces the fat content substantially.

Per serving

Calories 217
Sugars 26 g
Protein 16 g
Dietary fiber 3.5 g
Fats 6.6 g
Sodium 251 mg

Excellent source of vitamin A, Vitamin B12 and folic acid
Good source of vitamin C, magnesium and iron
Source of calcium and fiber

Québécois Shepherd's Pie

Tomato Meat Loaf

Try this loaf cold in a sandwich, on a baguette or a Kaiser bun with hot mustard.

PREPARATION: 10 MIN		COOKING TIME: 60 MIN	8 SERVINGS

500 g	lean ground beef	1 lb
125 ml	bulgur, uncooked	1/2 cup
75 ml	extra-old cheddar cheese, grated, or parmesan	1/3 cup
1	green onion, chopped	1
1	egg	1
45 ml	sun-dried tomatoes, rehydrated and chopped	3 Tbsp
15 ml	Worcestershire sauce	1 Tbsp
45 ml	parsley, chopped or 15 ml (1 Tbsp) dried parsley	3 Tbsp
2	cans (213 ml/7.5 oz) tomato sauce	2
1 ml	pepper	1/4 tsp
30 ml	brown sugar	2 Tbsp
5 ml	dry mustard	1 tsp

Preheat oven to 190°C (375°F).

In a bowl, mix beef, bulgur, cheese, green onion, egg, dried tomatoes, Worcestershire sauce, parsley and 1 can of tomato sauce. Put in a 28cm x 10cm (11" x 4") bread pan.

In another bowl, blend the second can of tomato sauce, pepper, brown sugar and dry mustard. Pour on the meat loaf. Cook in oven for 60 minutes or until a thermometer, inserted into the center of the loaf, reads 70°C (160°F).

Variation

Cook the mixture in muffin tins for individual servings. Reduce the cooking time to 25-30 minutes.

Tip

To rehydrate sun-dried tomatoes, soak them in boiling water for 15 minutes. Drain them, use them immediately, or cover them with olive oil and refrigerate.

Nutritional information

Adding the bulgur makes this dish go further. It is economizing on both money and fat content. Bulgur is the whole grain version of couscous. It is more nutritious and is particularly rich in niacin, magnesium and fiber.

Per serving

Calories 203
Sugars 15 g
Protein 17 g
Dietary fiber 2.5 g
Fats 8.8 g
Sodium 418 mg

Excellent source of vitamin B12
Good source of magnesium and iron
Source of vitamin A, folic acid, vitamin C, calcium and fiber

Desserts

Getting a healthy sugar fix is possible! The proof: these sweet treats you can enjoy at the end of lunch, as a snack, or after dinner.

Peanut Butter Cookies

Can be frozen

This is a different take on the traditional way to serve "peanut butter and jam".
Here is a dessert or snack that the peanut butter connoisseur will appreciate.

PREPARATION: 20 MIN		**COOKING TIME: 10 MIN**	**30 COOKIES**

200 ml	all-purpose flour	3/4 cup
125 ml	whole-wheat flour	1/2 cup
30 ml	cornstarch	2 Tbsp
5 ml	baking powder	1 tsp
2 ml	baking soda	1/2 tsp
2 ml	salt	1/2 tsp
50 ml	canola oil	1/4 cup
125 ml	brown sugar, lightly packed	1/2 cup
50 ml	corn syrup	1/4 cup
1	egg	1
50 ml	creamy peanut butter	1/4 cup
10 ml	vanilla	2 tsp
45 ml	sugar	3 Tbsp
50 ml	raspberry jam or jelly	1/4 cup

In a small bowl, mix the flours, corn starch, baking powder, baking soda and salt. Set aside.

In a large bowl, beat oil, brown sugar, corn syrup and egg with an electric mixer until it is homogenous. Beat in peanut butter and vanilla. Add dry ingredients and beat on low.

Form the dough into 2.5 cm (1") diameter balls. Roll them in the sugar and place them on a nonstick or oiled cookie sheet. Make an indentation with your thumb in the center of each cookie and garnish with 2 ml (1/2 tsp) jam or jelly.

Variation
Replace the jam with a candied cherry, a large chocolate chip, or a nut (almonds, filberts or walnuts).

Interesting fact
Peanut butter was invented in 1890 in the United States, but the Africans, North American Native people and Indonesians have prepared similar butters for a long time. For example, satay sauce, with a peanut base, is typically Indonesian.

Nutritional information
Peanuts, as well as having good monounsaturated fats (as has olive oil, hence its reputation as a healthy oil) is an economical source of protein and they provide nutrients that are in short supply in our North American diet.

Per serving
Calories 149
Sugars 26 g
Protein 2.1 g
Dietary fiber 0.9 g
Fats 4.2 g
Sodium 135 mg

Source of iron

Cranberry Bars

Ah cranberries, wonderful cranberries! Once dried, they can be eaten as candies! With their beautiful red color and slightly acid but sweet taste, they enhance this recipe of tender squares.

PREPARATION: 10 MIN	COOKING TIME: 20 MIN	20 SQUARES

250 ml	flour	1 cup
250 ml	large flake oats	1 cup
5 ml	baking powder	1 tsp
2 ml	salt	1/2 tsp
250 ml	brown sugar, lightly packed	1 cup
50 ml	canola oil	1/4 cup
2	eggs	2
250 ml	granola cereal with raisins, light mix	1 cup
200 ml	dried cranberries	3/4 cup

Preheat oven to 180°C (350°F).

Lightly oil a 23 x 33 cm (9" x 13") cake pan.

In a bowl, mix the flour, oats, baking powder and salt.

In a large bowl, beat with an electric mixer, the brown sugar, oil, and eggs until homogenous. Add the dry ingredients and beat on high.

Using a wooden spoon, fold in the granola and cranberries to this mixture (the mixture will be thick). Pour into the oiled pan.

Bake in oven 20-25 minutes or until top is slightly firm to the touch.

Let cool and cut into squares.

Variation
Replace dried cranberries with raisins, chopped dates, diced dried papaya or dried cherries.

Tip
You will usually find dried cherries at the supermarket along with the other dried fruits.

Per serving
Calories 147
Sugars 26 g
Protein 2.6 g
Dietary fiber 1.3 g
Fats 3.9 g
Sodium 84 mg

Source of iron

Granola Bars

Can be frozen

Always popular, these little treats are made with
nourishing whole grains, nuts and fruit!

| PREPARATION: 15 MIN | COOKING TIME: 30 MIN | 16 BARS |

Tip
When oat flakes are pan toasted, they take on a delicious nutty flavor. To toast, place oats on a cooking sheet and put in a preheated 180°C (350°F) oven just until oats are lightly browned or golden.

Interesting fact
Large flake oats are larger than rapid or minute oats. These oat forms have comparable nutritional value and are interchangeable in these recipes.

Nutritional information
These granola bars supply 5 essential nutrients and less fat and salt than commercial bars. To make even healthier bars, replace the chocolate chips with nuts or dried fruit.

Per serving
Calories 132
Sugars 25 g
Protein 2.5 g
Dietary fiber 1.3 g
Fats 3.5 g
Sodium 42 mg

Source of magnesium
and iron

Preheat oven to 160°C (325°F).

Oil a 20 x 28 cm (8" x 11") heat proof dish.

In a bowl, mix all the ingredients. Spread mixture evenly in the dish and cook for 30 minutes in the oven until top is golden.

Let cool and cut into bars.

2	eggs	2
250 ml	brown sugar, lightly packed	1 cup
15 ml	canola oil	1 Tbsp
15 ml	flour	1 Tbsp
5 ml	cinnamon	1 tsp
1 ml	salt	1/4 tsp
375 ml	toasted large flake oats	1 1/2 cup
75 ml	raisins	1/3 cup
75 ml	cranberries, apricots or other chopped dried fruit	1/3 cup
50 ml	semi-sweet chocolate chips	1/4 cup
50 ml	chopped pecan, slivered almonds, or toasted sunflower seeds	1/4 cup

Apple and Maple Syrup Crisp

A homemade delight with a crisp, fruity combination, this dessert tastes even better the next day (if there is any left!), when the apples have softened the oat topping.

PREPARATION: 15 MIN		COOKING TIME: 30 MIN	9 SQUARES

375 ml	flour	1 1/2 cups
250 ml	large flake oats	1 cup
200 ml	brown sugar or maple sugar, lightly packed	3/4 cup
3 ml	baking powder	3/4 tsp
2 ml	salt	1/2 tsp
2 ml	cinnamon	1/2 tsp
75 ml	maple syrup	5 Tbsp
45 ml	canola oil	3 Tbsp
2	large Cortland or Granny Smith apples or pears, peeled and sliced	2
50 ml	nuts, rough chopped	1/4 cup

Preheat oven to 180°C (350°F).

Lightly oil a 32 cm (9") square cake pan.

In a large bowl, mix the flour, oats, brown sugar, baking powder, salt and cinnamon. Mix in 45 ml (3 Tbsp) maple syrup and oil, using your fingers, until a rough texture is obtained.

Press 500 ml (2 cups) of this mixture in the bottom of the oiled cake pan. Place 3 rows of sliced apples on top.

Incorporate the nuts and remaining 30 ml (2 Tbsp) maple syrup into the rest of the flour mixture. Spread this on the layer of apples and press firmly to obtain a uniform layer.

Cook for 30-35 minutes or until the apples are cooked and the top is golden.

Let cool and cut into squares.

Advance preparation

Prepare 2-3 times the quantity of oat topping to freeze for later use.

Interesting fact

The apple orchard is the oldest and most widely planted of all the fruit orchards in Eastern Canada. The first orchard of New France was planted in 1650 on the slopes of Mount Royal by the Sulpiciens.

Nutritional information

Contrary to popular belief, apples are not an excellent source of vitamin C. However, they contain pectin which helps control cholesterol and blood sugar. In addition, apples clean the teeth and massage the gums.

Per serving

Calories 224
Sugars 37 g
Protein 4.4 g
Dietary fiber 2.4 g
Fats 7.5 g
Sodium 130 mg

Source of magnesium, iron and fiber

Jellied Fruit

This fruit gelatin is nourishing! Happily, it has enough body to support the trip from home to school.

PREPARATION: 5 MIN	WAITING TIME: 2 HOURS	16 SQUARES

Variation

Pour the liquid mixture directly into ramekins or small wide-mouth thermos containers. Add fruit pieces (peaches, pears, bananas) and let it set. Do not add kiwi or pineapple since they contain an enzyme which will prevent the gelatin from setting.

Nutritional information

Compared to commercial gelatins, this version contains more nutrients (such as vitamin C), a lot less salt and no coloring or artificial flavorings.

Per serving

Calories 56
Sugars 12 g
Protein 2.1 g
Dietary fiber 0 g
Fats 0.1 g
Sodium 4 mg

Source of vitamin C
Low in fat

Lightly oil a square cake pan 23 cm (9").

Pour water into a saucepan. Sprinkle with gelatin and let it swell for 1 minute. Heat saucepan on medium and bring to the boil, stirring frequently. Remove from heat. Add the fruit juice concentrate and mix just until it has melted.

Pour mixture in the oiled pan and refrigerate 2 hours or until the gelatin is firm.

Cut into squares with a knife or cutting mold.

375 ml	cold water	1 1/2 cups
4	packs (15 ml/1 Tbsp each) unflavored gelatin	4
1 can	(355 ml/12.5 oz) frozen concentrated fruit juice not diluted (apple, grape, orange)	1

Fruit-"Full" Muffins

These muffins filled with small fruits will remind you of the flavors of summer when the cold of winter sets in. They are also delicious prepared with frozen fruit.

PREPARATION: 10 MIN		COOKING TIME: 20 MIN	12 MUFFINS

250 ml	all-purpose flour	1 cup
250 ml	whole-wheat flour	1 cup
125 ml	wheat or oat bran	1/2 cup
5 ml	baking powder	1 tsp
2 ml	salt	1/2 tsp
2 ml	baking soda	1/2 tsp
50 ml	small dried fruit (cherries, blueberries or cranberries)	1/4 cup
1	egg	1
125 ml	brown sugar, lightly packed	1/2 cup
250 ml	buttermilk	1 cup
50 ml	canola oil	1/4 cup
10 ml	lemon zest	2 tsp
5 ml	vanilla	1 tsp
375 ml	mixed fresh fruit (raspberries, blueberries or blackberries)	1 1/2 cups
	Or 1 package (300 ml/10 oz) mixed frozen fruits – not defrosted	

Preheat oven to 200°C (400°F).

In a large bowl, mix the flour, bran, baking powder, salt, baking soda and dried fruit and set aside.

In a bowl, beat egg lightly and stir in brown sugar. Add buttermilk, oil, zest, vanilla and mix well. Make a well in the center of the dry ingredients and gently incorporate the liquid ingredients and fruits, stirring just until mixed.

Drop muffin mix by the spoonful into the nonstick or greased muffin tins.

Bake for 20-25 minutes or until muffins are firm to the touch.

Tip

The buttermilk can be replaced with the same amount of plain yogurt, or 250 ml (1 cup) milk with 15 ml (1 Tbsp) lemon juice or vinegar can be added. Let this mixture sit for 5 minutes before using it.

Nutritional information

Contrary to popular belief, buttermilk is not high in fat: it contains less than 1% fat. It is the whey that remains when cream is churned to produce butter. Since the milk sugar (lactose) has been converted to lactic acid, buttermilk has a sour taste and is easily digested by lactose-intolerant people.

Per muffin

Calories 160
Sugars 32 g
Protein 4.4 g
Dietary fiber 3.5 g
Fats 2.3 g
Sodium 211 mg

Source of vitamin B12, folic acid, vitamin C, magnesium, iron and fiber
Low in fat

Multi-Grain Prune Muffins

Can be frozen

Delectable muffins! They are filled with fiber and iron, nutrients often lacking in today's foods.

200 ml	all-purpose flour	3/4 cup
125 ml	whole-wheat flour	1/2 cup
125 ml	large flake oats	1/2 cup
125 ml	wheat germ	1/2 cup
75 ml	brown sugar, lightly packed	1/3 cup
7 ml	baking powder	1 1/2 tsp
5 ml	cinnamon	1 tsp
5 ml	orange zest	1 tsp
2 ml	baking soda	1/2 tsp
1	egg	1
250 ml	pitted prunes, chopped	1 cup
300 ml	plain yogurt	1 1/4 cup
45 ml	canola oil	3 Tbsp

Preheat oven to 200°C (400°F).

In a large bowl, mix the flours, oats, wheat germ, brown sugar, baking powder, cinnamon, zest, and baking soda. Set aside.

In a bowl, beat the egg lightly and add prunes, yogurt and oil. Make a well in the center of the dry ingredients and gently incorporate the liquid mixture, mixing just until dry ingredients are moist.

Pour the mixture into a nonstick or buttered muffin tin. Bake for 20-25 minutes or until muffins are firm to the touch.

Tips
As these muffins are low in oil, they could stick if paper muffin cups are used.

To lighten the traditional muffin recipe, replace half the oil with an equal amount of non-sweetened fruit sauce (apple sauce etc.).

Interesting fact
Most store-bought muffins are made with white flour and contain 350-450 calories and 10-20 g (2-4 tsp) of fat!

Per muffin
Calories 198
Sugars 34 g
Protein 5.7 g
Dietary fiber 3.3g
Fats 5.2 g
Sodium 117 mg

Good source of magnesium
Source of vitamin B12, folic acid, calcium, iron and fiber

Cherry and Almond Scones

The delicious aroma of these almond flavored scones guard a secret that is up to us to keep: they contain tofu!

Can be frozen

PREPARATION: 10 MIN	COOKING TIME: 15 MIN	12 SCONES

Variation

Replace cherries with the same quantity of finely slivered dried apricots.

Per scone

Calories 136
Sugars 27 g
Protein 3.8 g
Dietary fiber 2.1 g
Fats 1.9 g
Sodium 217 mg

Source of magnesium, iron and fiber
Low in fat

In a large bowl, mix the flours, sugar, baking powder, salt, cardamom, baking soda, cherries and almonds.

In a large measuring cup, purée the tofu with a hand mixer and add the milk until you have 400 ml (1 2/3 cups) of liquid.

Make a well in the center of dry ingredients. Add liquids and stir just until the dry ingredients are moist.

By large spoonfuls, place the dough on a nonstick or oiled baking sheet. Sprinkle with sugar.

Bake 15 minutes or until the scones are golden.

375 ml	all-purpose flour	1 1/2 cups
200 ml	whole-wheat flour	3/4 cup
30 ml	sugar	2 Tbsp
15 ml	baking powder	1 Tbsp
2 ml	salt	1/2 tsp
2 ml	cardamom or cinnamon	1/2 tsp
2 ml	baking soda	1/2 tsp
125 ml	dried cherries	1/2 cup
50 ml	slivered almonds, toasted	1/4 cup
1	pkg (300 g/10 oz) soft tofu, almond flavored	1
15 ml	sugar	1 Tbsp

Chocolate Pudding

A favorite with the small fry! Pudding is always good!

200 ml	sugar	3/4 cup
3	eggs	3
125 ml	corn starch	1/2 cup
1 L	milk	4 cups
5 ml	vanilla	1 tsp
2	semi-sweet chocolate squares, melted	2

In a bowl, mix sugar, eggs, and corn starch and set aside. In a heavy bottomed saucepan, heat the milk until it is steaming (just below the boiling point).

Pour hot milk, a little at a time, into the egg mixture to heat it, and stir after each addition.

Pour this mixture into the saucepan and heat, stirring constantly, until thickened. Incorporate the vanilla and melted chocolate squares.

Pour into 8 individual 200 ml (3/4 cup) bowls.

Variation

Place banana slices or diced pears in individual bowls before pouring in the pudding. Omit the chocolate squares for a vanilla pudding version.

Nutritional information

Compared to store-bought puddings, this version contains twice as much vitamin A and folic acid and five times less sodium.

Per serving

Calories 230
Sugars 40 g
Protein 6.9 g
Dietary fiber 0.4 g
Fats 5.3 g
Sodium 90 mg

Excellent source of vitamin B12
Good source of calcium
Source of vitamin A, folic acid and magnesium

Super Chocolate Cake

Can be frozen

The kids will ask for more! The Dutch cocoa gives a flavor and velvety touch to this unpretentious, nutritional chocolate delight.

PREPARATION: 15 MIN	WAITING TIME: 10 MIN	COOKING TIME: 35 MIN	9 SERVINGS

Tip

Dutch chocolate gives a darker color than American chocolate. Compared to bitter chocolate which contains between 52-56% fat, cocoa only contains between 10-24% fat.

Nutritional information

Cardamom possesses a warm, lightly peppery flavor. It can replace ginger or cinnamon in most recipes.

Per serving

Calories 169
Sugars 29 g
Protein 7.1 g
Dietary fiber 1.1 g
Fats 3.6 g
Sodium 153 mg

Good source of calcium
Source of vitamin A, vitamin B12, folic acid, vitamin C, magnesium and iron

Preheat oven to 180°C (350°F).

Lightly oil a 23 cm (9") square cake tin. Spread bread crumbs evenly on bottom of pan.

In a large bowl, beat the eggs well and beat in milk, brown sugar, cocoa, vanilla and cardamom. Pour mixture on the bread, and to facilitate absorption, prick with a fork until liquid is absorbed. Layer with chocolate chips and almonds. Let sit 10 minutes.

Bake 35 minutes or until the center is puffed and cooked.

1 L	stale bread, torn into small bits	4 cups
2	eggs	2
1	can (385 ml/14 oz) evaporated skim milk	1
125 ml	brown sugar, lightly packed	1/2 cup
50 ml	cocoa, preferably Dutch cocoa	1/4 cup
10 ml	vanilla	2 tsp
1	pinch of cardamom or cinnamon	1
30 ml	semi-sweet chocolate chips	2 Tbsp
30 ml	almonds, toasted slivered	2 Tbsp

Orange Pumpkin Bread

So simple to prepare using canned puréed pumpkin!

PREPARATION: 10 MIN	**COOKING TIME: 60 MIN**	**14 SLICES 2 CM (3/4") THICK**

250 ml	whole-wheat flour	1 cup
150 ml	all-purpose flour	2/3 cup
7 ml	cinnamon	1 1/2 tsp
5 ml	baking soda	1 tsp
2 ml	baking powder	1/2 tsp
2 ml	cardamom	1/2 tsp
1 ml	salt	1/4 tsp
	zest of 1 orange	
200 ml	dates, chopped	3/4 cup
75 ml	canola oil	1/3 cup
2 ml	vanilla	1/2 tsp
150 ml	sugar	2/3 cup
2	eggs	2
250 ml	pumpkin purée	1 cup
75 ml	orange juice	1/3 cup

Preheat oven to 180°C (350°F).

Oil and flour a 10 x 28 cm (4" x 11") bread pan. In a large bowl, mix flours, cinnamon, baking soda, baking powder, cardamom, salt, zest, dates and set aside.

In a smaller bowl, beat oil, vanilla and sugar. Add eggs and mix well. Stir in pumpkin purée and orange juice. Make a well in the center of the dry ingredients and pour in the liquid ingredients, stirring just until the mixture is combined. Pour into the prepared bread pan.

Bake for 60 minutes or until a toothpick inserted in the center comes out clean. Remove from oven and let rest 10 minutes before turning out onto a wire rack. Let cool.

Tips

To facilitate lunch making, slice the bread, seal in separate pieces and freeze. You can easily double this recipe.

For variety, pour the batter into muffin tins. Baking time will be approximately 20 minutes at 200°C (400°F).

Per serving

Calories 175
Sugars 29 g
Protein 3.1 g
Dietary fiber 2.5 g
Fats 5.9 g
Sodium 153 mg

Excellent source of vitamin A
Source of folic acid, vitamin C, magnesium, iron and fiber

Orange Pumpkin Bread

Chocolate Banana Loaf

With this recipe, there is no excuse for throwing away ripe bananas!

PREPARATION: 10 MIN	COOKING TIME: 60 MIN	14 SLICES 2 CM (3/4") THICK

250 ml	ripe banana, mashed	1 cup
50 ml	canola oil	1/4 cup
50 ml	milk	1/4 cup
2	eggs	2
250 ml	all-purpose flour	1 cup
250 ml	whole-wheat flour	1 cup
200 ml	sugar	3/4 cup
10 ml	baking powder	2 tsp
1 ml	salt	1/4 tsp
125 ml	semi-sweet chocolate chips	1/2 cup
50 ml	sliced almonds, toasted	1/4 cup

Preheat oven to 180°C (350°F). Oil and lightly flour a 10 x 28 cm (4" x 11") loaf pan.

In a bowl, mix together banana, oil, milk and eggs. Set aside.

In a large bowl, mix remaining ingredients. Fold liquid mixture into dry ingredients, stirring just until mixture is combined. Pour into oiled loaf pan.

Bake 60 minutes or until a toothpick inserted in the center of the cake comes out clean. Remove from oven and let rest 10 minutes before turning out onto a wire rack.

Tip

If you have ripe bananas but not enough time to make this recipe, freeze the bananas, skin on. When they are defrosted they will be soft and have a perfect flavor, ideal for cakes, cookies and muffins.

Per slice

Calories 209
Sugars 34 g
Protein 4.0 g
Dietary fiber 1.8 g
Fats 7.2 g
Sodium 98 mg

Source of vitamin B12, folic acid, magnesium and iron

Beverages

Refreshing, thirst quenching and nourishing, these flavorful and colorful beverages are ready in a few moments!

Mango Batido

This Cuban milk and mango-based beverage is the color of the sun!

PREPARATION: 10 MIN		3 SERVINGS 250 ML (1 CUP)

1	mango, cubed	1
250 ml	milk	1 cup
125 ml	plain yogurt	1/2 cup
30 ml	skim milk powder	2 Tbsp
15 ml	maple syrup	1 Tbsp
	pinch of cardamom or cinnamon	
4	ice cubes (optional)	4

Purée mango pulp in the blender until it is smooth. Add the rest of the ingredients. Mix until blended.

Serve immediately or refrigerate to chill.

Variation
Replace mango with a can (398 ml/14 oz) of peaches, drained, or with 250 ml (1 cup) purée made with ripe fruits (peaches, pears, bananas).

Tip
If the mango is very fibrous, strain the drink through a fine sieve.

Interesting fact
A mango can be chosen with your eyes closed! Don't go by the color to ascertain whether the mango is ripe, but by its sweet odor, and when pressed lightly with the fingers, the flesh will give a little. If it is not sufficiently ripe, leave it at room temperature for a few days.

Per serving
Calories 143
Sugars 26 g
Protein 7.3 g
Dietary fiber 1.4 g
Fats 1.8 g
Sodium 103 mg

Excellent source of
vitamin A and vitamin B12
Good source of vitamin C
and calcium
Source of folic acid
and magnesium
Low in fat

"Whiplash" Shake

An invigorating, velvety "chocolate-banana" blend.

PREPARATION: 5 MIN

2 SERVINGS 250 ML (1 CUP)

Interesting fact

You can add eggs or egg whites into a non-cooked food if they are pasteurized (commercial liquid whole eggs or whites). Pasteurization eliminates the risk of salmonella contamination when using raw eggs.

Per serving

Calories 301
Sugars 45 g
Protein 16 g
Dietary fiber 1.5 g
Fats 7.9 g
Sodium 223 mg

Excellent source of vitamin B12, folic acid, magnesium and calcium
Good source of vitamin A
Source of vitamin C and iron

Mix all ingredients in blender until smooth.

250 ml	milk	1 cup
1	banana	1
30 ml	chocolate malt powder (like Ovaltine)	2 Tbsp
30 ml	skim milk powder	2 Tbsp
15 ml	wheat germ	1 Tbsp
2	eggs	2

The Morning "Blues"

Nothing better than beginning your day in color!

PREPARATION: 5 MIN

2 SERVINGS 200 ML (3/4 CUP)

250 ml	buttermilk	1 cup
200 ml	frozen blueberries	3/4 cup
15 ml	skim milk powder	1 Tbsp
15 ml	brown sugar	1 Tbsp

Blend all ingredients in blender until smooth.

Variation

For a "psychedelic" version, freeze puréed blueberries, raspberries or strawberries in freezer trays. Put them in a glass of buttermilk and let them melt slowly while stirring, to obtain interesting colors.

Interesting fact

The red pigment, anthocyanin, which gives blueberries their lovely color, are antioxidants which protect against heart disease and cancer. A good reason to "eat blue"!

Per serving

Calories 127
Sugars 24 g
Protein 6.1 g
Dietary fiber 1.6 g
Fats 1.4 g
Sodium 162 mg

Good source of
vitamin B12 and calcium
Source of folic acid,
vitamin C and magnesium
Low in fat

The Morning "Blues"   Mango Batido   "Whiplash" Shake

Pineapple Milk Shake

A relaxing sun-drenched beverage.

250 ml	crushed pineapple	1 cup
125 ml	milk	1/2 cup
125 ml	ice cream or frozen vanilla yogurt	1/2 cup

Blend all ingredients in blender until smooth.

Interesting fact

The Spaniards named the pineapple *pina* because it resembles a pine cone. The English language retained this reference and called it *pineapple*.

Nutritional information

Canned pineapple can be used in a gelatin mixture or milk without a problem because the heat used in the canning process kills bromelain, a natural enzyme in fresh pineapple. Bromelain tenderizes meat, prevents gelatin from setting, and sours milk.

Per serving

Calories 175
Sugars 32 g
Protein 3.9 g
Dietary fiber 1.2 g
Fats 4.6 g
Sodium 62 mg

Good source of vitamin B12
Source of vitamin A, folic acid, vitamin C, magnesium and calcium

Orange and Almond
Tofu Shake

A good taste of almonds and the goodness of tofu, quickly prepared.

Per serving

Calories 248
Sugars 35 g
Protein 11 g
Dietary fiber 1.7 g
Fats 7.5 g
Sodium 53 mg

Good source of
vitamin B12, folic acid,
vitamin C and magnesium
Source of calcium

Blend all ingredients in blender until smooth.

1	pkg (300 g/10 oz) soft tofu almond flavored	1
15 ml	sugar	1 Tbsp
125 ml	orange juice	1/2 cup
30 ml	ground almonds	2 Tbsp
30 ml	skim milk powder	2 Tbsp

Four weeks of menus

Short of ideas? Seasonal menus, ethnic menus, vegetarian menus, holiday menus … these can be added to your repertoire! All these menus are made up of foods from at least three of the four food groups.

Week 1

Monday
A piecemeal lunch

Ideal for meals taken on the run.

Box of tomato juice
Rice cakes
Hard cooked egg
String cheese
Roasted soy nut snack
Banana

Tuesday
The Italian way!

Minestrone (p. 62) or
Fennel and orange salad (p. 94)
Onion and gorgonzola pizza
(p. 131)
Biscotti

Wednesday
It's Autumn!

Forestière quiche (p. 136)
Celery root salad with orange
dressing (p. 103)
Peach crisp
Milk box

Thursday
For brunch and/or lunch

Can be eaten once or twice…

Crunchy cheese spread (p. 121)
on an English muffin, or
Muesli cereal with plain yogurt
Peanut dip (p. 80) with fresh
fruit chunks
Orange and almond tofu shake
(p. 179)

Friday
Picnic on the lawn

**The only things missing are a knife
and spoon and a checkered
tablecloth!**

Baguette or whole-wheat crackers
Flaked tuna with lemon and
pepper (store-bought)
Black or green olives
Brie triangle
Whole nuts
Grapes and strawberries
Frozen juice box*

* If it is not completely defrosted at
  meal time, cut off the box top and
  eat the contents with a spoon as
  a sorbet

Week 2

Monday
The children cook

**They can prepare this food
themselves during the weekend.**

Bag of baby carrots
Crusty chicken nuggets (p. 150)
Cabbage salad (store-bought)
Super chocolate cake (p. 169)
Milk box

Tuesday
A break from meat!

Veggie-burger (p. 128) or millet
or seitan paté (store-bought)
Crunchy vegetables seasoned
with balsamic vinegar (p. 95)
or legume salad (store-bought)
Fruit-"Full" muffins (p. 164)

Wednesday
Who wants soup?

Creamed clam and fennel
soup (p. 61) or
Chowder (ready-to-eat,
store-bought)
Croutons or crackers
Green salad, sprayed with oil
and lemon juice
Cherry and almond scones
(p. 167)

Thursday
Taste of the Middle East

Middle-East salad (p. 105) or
Mint carrot salad (p. 102)
Quick shish taouk sandwich
(p. 117) or
Lebanese samosas (p. 148)
Clementine orange
Kefir

Friday
Sugar cabin lunch

A first taste of spring!

Paté and country bread
Roasted lentils (p. 91) or
Beans in tomato sauce
(store-bought)
Slice of ham
Apple and maple syrup crisp
(p. 162)
with a slice of cheddar cheese

Week 3

Monday
The children cook

They can prepare this food themselves during the weekend.

Vegetable dip (store-bought) or
Avocado mayonnaise (p. 75)
Veggies (cherry tomatoes, cauliflower, broccoli)
Tuna wrap (p. 114)
Peanut butter cookies (p. 158)

Tuesday
Chinese fare

Vietnamese chicken soup (p. 70) or
Asian chicken stir-fry (p. 152)
White rice
Tutti frutti salad with poppy seed sauce (p. 112)
Fortune cookies
Enriched soy milk

Wednesday
Winter comfort

Vegetable juice
Duo colored potato gratin dauphinois (p. 88) and
Tomato meat loaf (p. 156) or
Québécois shepherd's pie (p. 154)
Green salad
Granola bar (p. 161)

Thursday
Sport menu

Perfect for a day in the fresh air!

Carrot and red pepper sticks
Red lentil and bulgur pilaf (p. 92)
Multi-grain prune muffins (p. 166)
Tube yogurt
Orange
Bottled water

Friday
It's Halloween!

Good enough for our little pranksters!

Toad juice (Emerald soup p. 64)
Witch's stew (Moroccan fruit casserole p. 153 or
Spiced chick pea ragout p. 90)
Orange flavored pumpkin bread (p. 170) and
'snake venom' (apple sauce, store-bought)

Week 4

Monday
A piecemeal lunch

Ideal for last minute lunches or lunch on the run.

Cherry tomatoes
Bagel
Pack of mixed nuts
Drinkable yogurt
Apple

Tuesday
A low-cal meal
500 calories

Chicken and mango sandwich (p. 118)
Melon and cucumber salad (p. 96)
Jellied fruit (p. 163)
Milk box

Wednesday
A break from meat!

Green salad with sweet red pepper dressing (p. 84)
Macaroni with all the trimmings! (p. 143) or
Bean burritos (frozen, store-bought) or
Alfre-tofu fettucini (p. 141)
Rice or tapioca pudding (store-bought)

Thursday
Kids Cuisine

The children cook to keep them busy when homework is finished!

Cantaloupe balls and fresh mint, balsamic vinegar
Kiddies confetti rice (p. 134)
Cheese curds
Cranberry bar (p. 160)

Friday
Olé Olé menu

Quick tex-mex consommé (p. 60)
Rice and black bean Mexican salad (p. 99)
Tomato slices
Tortilla or corn crackers, oven toasted
Mango batido (p. 174)

Servings with respect to
Canada's Food Guide

Servings with respect to

	Grain products	Vegetables and fruits	Milk products	Meats and alternatives
Soups				
Quick tex-mex consommé	1/2	1	0	0
Creamed clam and fennel soup	0	1	1/2	1/2
Minestrone	1/2	1	0	1/4
Broccoli and apple soup	0	1 1/2	1/2	0
Emerald soup	0	1 1/2	1/4	0
Beef and barley soup	1/2	1 1/2	0	1/2
Mexican meatball soup	1/2	2	0	1
Orange lentil soup	0	1 1/2	0	1/4
Chicken noodle soup	1/2	1	0	1
Vietnamese chicken soup (Pho Ga)	1/2	1 1/2	0	1
Tortellini and spinach soup	1/2	2	1/4	0
Dressings, dips and sauces				
Hummus	0	0	0	0
Avocado mayonnaise	0	0	0	0
Lemon mayonnaise	0	0	0	0
Sweet and sour sauce	0	1/4	0	0
Remoulade sauce	0	0	0	0
Mushroom dip	0	1/4	0	0
Peanut dip	0	0	0	1/4
Cranberry dressing	0	1/4	0	0
Pizzaiolla dressing	0	1/4	0	0
Sweet red pepper dressing	0	0	0	0
Thousand Island dressing	0	0	0	0

	Grain products	Vegetables and fruits	Milk products	Meats and alternatives
Vegetables, legumes and salads				
Duo colored potato gratin dauphinois	1/4	1	1/2	0
Spiced chick pea ragout	0	1 1/2	0	1/2
Roasted lentils	0	1/2	0	1
Red lentil and bulgur pilaf	1	1/2	0	1/2
Fennel and orange salad	0	1	0	0
Crunchy vegetables seasoned with balsamic vinegar	0	1 1/2	0	0
Melon and cucumber salad	0	2	0	0
"Quills" and chicken with fruit and curry	2	1	1/4	1
New potatoes with lemon-chive vinaigrette	0	3	0	0
Rice and black bean Mexican salad	3/4	1	0	1/2
Tofu Greek salad	1/2	3	1/4	1/2
Mint carrot salad	0	1 1/2	0	0
Celery root salad with orange dressing	0	2	0	0
Lentil salad	0	1/2	1/2	1
Middle-East salad	1	1	0	1/2
Tuna pasta salad with sweet pepper dressing	2	1	0	1/2
Tortellini salad with sun-dried tomato sauce	1	2	1/2	0
Multi-colored salad – two methods	0	2	0	0
Tri-colored salad	0	2	0	1/2
Waldorf salad	0	1	0	0
Tutti frutti salad with poppy seed sauce	0	2	0	0
Breads, pizzas, sandwiches and garnishes				
Tuna wrap	1	0	0	1/2
Grilled chicken sandwich with caramelized onions	2	1	0	1

	Grain products	Vegetables and fruits	Milk products	Meats and alternatives
Quick shish taouk sandwich	2	1/2	0	1
Chicken and mango chutney sandwich	2	1/2	0	1/2
Grilled apple and cheese sandwich	2	1/2	1/2	0
Crunchy cheese spread	0	1/4	0	0
Pan-bagnat sandwich	2	1	0	1
Tomato parsley	0	1/4	0	0
Egg sandwich	2	1/4	0	1/2
Roast beef emperadado	2	1/2	0	1/2
Veggie burgers	1/2	1/2	0	1/4
Italian Quesadillas	2	1	1	0
Black olive, parmesan, and pine nut scones	11/2	0	1/4	0
Onion and gorgonzola pizza	11/2	1/2	1/4	0
Pizza pockets	2	1	1/2	1/4

Eggs and pasta

	Grain products	Vegetables and fruits	Milk products	Meats and alternatives
Kiddies confetti rice	1/2	0	0	1/2
Forestière quiche	1	1	0	1/2
Spanish tortilla	0	1	0	1
Artichoke and parmesan frittata	0	1	0	1/2
Italian pasta omelet	1	1	0	1
Alfre-tofu fettucini	3	0	1/4	1
Macaroni and cheese "secret code"	2	1/2	1/4	1/2
Macaroni with all the trimmings	11/2	2	0	1
Mamma mia polenta	1	11/2	1/4	1
Cheese and onion pasta	2	1	11/2	0

Chicken and beef

	Grain products	Vegetables and fruits	Milk products	Meats and alternatives
Lebanese samosas	2	1/2	0	1/2
Crusty chicken nuggets	1/4	0	0	1
Quick egg rolls	2	1/2	0	1/4

	Grain products	Vegetables and fruits	Milk products	Meats and alternatives
Asian chicken stir-fry	0	21/2	0	1
Moroccan fruit casserole	0	21/2	0	1
Québécois shepherd's pie	0	2	0	1
Tomato meat loaf	1/2	1/2	0	1

Desserts

	Grain products	Vegetables and fruits	Milk products	Meats and alternatives
Peanut butter cookies	1/2	0	0	0
Cranberry bars	1/2	1/4	0	0
Granola bars	1/4	1/4	0	0
Apple and maple syrup crisp	11/2	1/4	0	0
Jellied fruit	0	3/4	0	0
Fruit-"Full" muffins	1	1/4	0	0
Multi-grain prune muffins	1	1/2	0	0
Cherry and almond scones	1	1/4	0	1/4
Chocolate pudding	0	0	1/2	0
Super chocolate cake	1/2	0	1/4	0
Orange pumpkin bread	3/4	1/2	0	0
Chocolate banana loaf	1	0	0	0

Beverages

	Grain products	Vegetables and fruits	Milk products	Meats and alternatives
Mango batido	0	1/2	3/4	0
"Whiplash" shake	1/4	1	1	1
The morning "blues"	0	1/2	1/2	0
Pineapple milk shake	0	1	1/2	0
Orange and almond tofu shake	0	1/2	1/4	1

Index